GREAT AME...

DREW BREES

MATT CHRISTOPHER

Little, Brown and Company
New York Boston

Little, Brown and Company

Hachette Book Group
1290 Avenue of the Americas, New York, NY 10104
Visit us at lb-kids.com

mattchristopher.com

Little, Brown and Company is a division of Hachette Book Group, Inc.
The Little, Brown name and logo are trademarks of Hachette Book Group, Inc.

The publisher is not responsible for websites (or their content) that are not owned by the publisher.

First Edition: December 2015

Matt Christopher® is a registered trademark of Matt Christopher Royalties, Inc.

Written by Zachary Rau
Cover illustration by Michael Cho

Library of Congress Cataloging-in-Publication Data

Christopher, Matt, 1917–1997.
Great Americans in sports, Drew Brees / Matt Christopher. — First Edition.
pages cm
"Written by Zachary Rau"—T.p. verso.
Audience: Age: 8–12.
ISBN 978-0-316-29666-3 (trade paperback) — ISBN 978-0-316-29667-0 (ebook) — ISBN 978-0-316-29665-6 (library edition ebook) 1. Brees, Drew, 1979– —Juvenile literature. 2. Football players—United States—Biography—Juvenile literature. 3. Quarterbacks (Football)—United States—Biography—Juvenile literature. I. Title.
GV939.B695C57 2015
796.332092—dc23
[B]
2015020887

10 9 8 7 6 5 4 3 2 1

RRD-C

Printed in the United States of America

CONTENTS

INTRODUCTION

Football is, perhaps, the ultimate team sport. With sixty minutes on the clock, eleven warriors take the field to face eleven warriors. Everyone on the field has a role to play, and everyone has a job to do. Every action is choreographed, and every play carefully planned. If any of the eleven players fails, the team might fail.

Even so, while there are twenty-one other players on the field at any given moment, there is one who stands out. That player's job alone sets him apart from every other player on the field—and that player is the quarterback. The quarterback could be considered the most important player on the football field. In fact, quarterbacks are often called field generals or game managers. In professional sports, few players face as much pressure as the quarterback of an NFL team.

What sets the position apart is not simply the pressure, the media attention, or the fans' expectations, of which there are certainly plenty. It is not the fact that the quarterback is the only one who has to know where every other player on the field is at all times, or the countless hours of study that it takes to prepare for a single game. It is not the intelligence the position requires, nor is it the focus. It isn't the leadership on and off the field. It isn't the ability to make quick decisions, or read defenses, or recover from a misstep. It isn't that a quarterback has to have the strength to throw a ball the length of a football field or be accurate enough to knock the wings off a fly in midair. It isn't just one of these qualities—to play quarterback, an athlete must have them all. Quarterbacks need to have a set of physical tools, as well as a unique education and strong understanding of the game. This is what makes the position so hard to scout, and why so few prospects become successful quarterbacks.

The prototypical NFL quarterback is somewhere between six feet two inches and six feet five inches tall and weighs 220 to 235 pounds. The popular opinion has always been that a quarterback shorter than six feet one inch can't see over his offensive line, which typically stands in front of him and consists of large players whose jobs are to block the other team from tackling the quarterback, the running back, the tight end, and the wide receiver.

Despite the common school of thought that quarterbacks must be tall in order to see the whole field, some quarterbacks have proved they can use passing lanes to see their receivers. They have shown that throwing the ball over the offensive line is more about a quarterback's release point and how high the ball is when it is thrown. Still, a stigma often stands around the height of quarterbacks. Most general managers and coaches will not take a chance on a "short" quarterback—and when someone does take a chance on him, that player must prove himself at every turn.

From the time he got the chance to start in high school, however, one quarterback in particular has challenged the idea of how tall or big a quarterback should be. Standing at only six feet tall, Drew Brees has climbed to the top of the NFL, where he remains one of the most talented, successful, and popular quarterbacks to this day.

CHAPTER ONE
1950–1977

TEXAS PEDIGREE

Vince Lombardi, the famous former coach, once said, "Football is a great deal like life in that it teaches that work, sacrifice, perseverance, competitive drive, selflessness, and respect for authority is the price that each and every one of us must pay to achieve any goal that is worthwhile." Nowhere is this truer than in the great state of Texas. In most Texan towns, Friday nights are reserved for football. Stores close early, the downtown streets empty, and there is a glow in the sky on the distant horizon— the glow of Friday night lights.

The legendary high school football coach Ray Akins knew what it was like to stand in the glow of those Friday night lights. After serving in the marines during World War II and fighting in Okinawa, Japan, Akins returned to Texas and coached for the better part of four decades, including an amazing run at Gregory-Portland Independent School

District from 1965 until he retired in 1988. He won around three hundred games during his twenty-three-year career at Gregory-Portland, and even led a team quarterbacked by his son all the way to the 1971 State Finals, where they unfortunately lost the championship game by just one point. Ray Akins was inducted into the Texas Sports Hall of Fame in 1992. But that's not his only claim to fame: he also happens to be Drew Brees's maternal grandfather.

Following the success of the 1971 Gregory-Portland team, colleges heavily recruited Ray's son, Marty. During a recruiting visit to South Bend, Indiana, Marty fell in love with the University of Notre Dame. He was strongly considering becoming a Fighting Irish before the realities of his father's job became clear to him. Ray would not be able to attend any of Marty's games if he went to school out of state. There was too much to do to prepare for those high school football games in Texas. Ray, however, made it clear that he would support his son in whatever decision he made.

"I'll never forget my dad saying, 'I'm a high school football coach, and you know how Friday nights are and how we spend Saturday mornings planning for the next game,'" Marty Akins said. "He said, 'I'll never get to see you play one college football game if you go to Notre Dame. But if that's where you want to go, that's great.'"

He would, of course, watch every one of Marty's games on television, but he would not be able to make the trip from the southern coast of Texas to northern Indiana and back in one day, and still get all his work done. For Marty, that was a game changer. He wanted his mother and father to have the chance to come to his games and watch him play, so Marty took a visit with the University of Texas at Austin.

While Marty had played for Gregory-Portland, his father was harder on him than on any other player. They studied the game and watched tapes of games all the time. They talked defensive schemes and ways to break them down offensively. He was a true student of football. After Marty's visit, University of Texas head coach Darrell Royal knew he had found his quarterback of the future. Marty was big, tough, and knew the game well enough to adjust to Coach Royal's wishbone offense, which is when the quarterback must either pitch the ball to the running back or run the ball, rather than throwing it.

"I ran the ball in high school, but mostly I threw

the ball," Marty remembered. "Coming to Texas and running the wishbone was something new for me." This adjustment required a quarterback who wasn't afraid to take a hit and was humble enough to play within the system.

Coach Royal wanted Marty Akins to be his quarterback at Texas, and once Marty decided he wanted to play close to home, he knew he was going to be a Longhorn at the University of Texas at Austin. It didn't hurt that Coach Royal brought former president Lyndon B. Johnson to the recruiting meeting with the Akins family.

"Here I was, a high school kid, sitting down with President Johnson," Marty recalled. "He was bigger than life. He seemed like a giant of a person to me."

Marty was sold! He committed to play for the Texas Longhorns.

Marty Akins arrived in Austin as a freshman in the fall of 1972 and spent his first season as the backup quarterback. He learned everything he could from Coach Royal and starter Alan Lowry while the Longhorns went 10–1, ending the season as the third ranked team in the Associated Press poll.

It didn't take long for Marty to win the starting spot, and by the spring practices of his first year, he was QB-One. During his second season, he piloted Texas to a sixth consecutive Southwest Conference title with an 8–3 overall record and 7–0 in the Southwest Conference. Unfortunately for Marty, his first season as a starter ended with a bad 19–3 loss to twelfth-ranked Nebraska in the 1974 Cotton Bowl Classic.

He was in his final season, in 1975, when he really proved his tough spirit. In the second-to-last game of the year, the Longhorns hosted Texas Christian University in a fateful game that would change the Longhorns' season. The Texas Christian University Horned Frogs had yet to win a game that season and were considered the heavy underdogs. In other words, TCU was a team that Texas should have easily beaten. However, the landscape of that game changed for the Longhorns when Marty tore the anterior cruciate ligament (ACL) in his knee. It was a horrible injury that forced him out of the game—and could have permanently ended his career. Texas managed a win against the Horned Frogs, but Marty's injury had left the Longhorns with a big hole.

The last game of the regular season was against the Longhorns' rival Texas A&M on November 28, 1975. A win would clinch the Southwest Conference

Championship, but a loss would mean they would have to share the title. After the injury in the TCU game, most fans expected Marty Akins to be out for the rest of the season. A tear to that particular ligament was a season-ending knee injury to any other player—but Marty wasn't like any other player.

"You've got to be a tough person because you are going to get hit on every play and, through the season, you are going to receive injuries to your elbows, wrists, your knees, your shoulders," Marty said. "I played with all kinds of injuries those four years at Texas."

Marty strapped on a knee brace and limped out onto the field to face Texas A&M's Aggies. But after the first play, he knew his leg just wasn't right and that it would be a mistake to go on with an injured knee. The coach took him off the field, but Marty argued to come back once again later in the game. His leg didn't work for more than a few plays, however, and by the second quarter, his night was over.

The University of Texas would lose that game 20–10. The loss meant that they had to share the Southwest Conference championship with Arkansas and Texas A&M. It was a bitter disappointment. Still, their overall year was successful enough that they earned an invitation to the Astro-Bluebonnet Bowl against Colorado. Marty spent a lot of time rehabilitating his leg, and after a rocky start to their Bowl game, Marty and the Longhorns would go on to own the second half and win 38–21. It was a great way for Marty to finish his season—and his college career!

Marty Akins would end his time at Texas with four school records, including most rushing yards by a quarterback (2,020), most rushing touchdowns by a quarterback (26), and most quarterback starts (34), while winning the Southwest Conference championship in 1973 and 1975 for a career record of 25–9. In 1975, he was an All-American selection.

After the season, Akins was drafted by the St. Louis Cardinals in the eleventh round of the 1976 NFL draft. He would then be traded to the New Orleans Saints in 1977, before hanging up his cleats for good that year and becoming a lawyer. He was inducted into the Texas Sports Hall of Fame in 1987. Ray and Marty Akins are the only father and son to have been inducted into the Texas Sports Hall of Fame. But soon enough there would be a new family member stepping onto the Texas football field— Ray's grandson and Marty's nephew: Drew Brees.

CHAPTER TWO
1979–1992

THE SEEDS OF DISCIPLINE

With the connection to Ray and Marty, Drew Brees was born into an athletic family. But Drew's grandfather and uncle weren't the only athletes in the family. Drew's father, Eugene Wilson "Chip" Brees II, played basketball at Texas A&M. His mother, Mina Akins, the daughter of Ray and sister to Marty, was All-State in basketball and volleyball. Most important, Drew was born into a family of intelligent hard workers who valued character and discipline above all else.

Chip and Mina welcomed their first-born son, Andrew Christopher Brees, to the world on January 15, 1979. Drew took to sports early in his life. As boys, Drew and his brother, Reid, who was two years younger, would spend their summers on their grandfather Ray's ranch. While Ray Akins ran the

Gregory-Portland football team in the sweltering Texas heat, Drew and Reid acted as ball boys and would fetch water for the players.

"During two-a-days, we'd go out there, and my grandpa would serve this green electrolyte water—it was kind of funky—and we'd be over there, me and my brother, filling them up and giving them to the guys and tossing the ball on the side and just thought that was the greatest thing ever, being a part of that and watching Grandpa coach and going to his games," Drew said.

It was during these summers that Ray Akins's never-give-up values rubbed off on Drew and planted the seeds for the player he would become in high school, college, and the pros. Drew has said of his grandfather that "some of my best memories as a kid are with him and my grandmother." Whether it was hunting, fishing, or just helping with the chores on the ranch, Ray Akins never missed an opportunity to teach, coach, and encourage his grandsons.

Growing up in Austin, Texas, Drew's favorite sport was baseball, but he liked all sports. "My brother and I were just sports junkies. Every free second we had was out in the yard playing tennis or running around," he recalled.

The boys were in elementary school when their parents decided to get a divorce. It was undoubtedly a hard transition for Drew—and sports helped make it that much easier.

CHAPTER THREE
1993–1995

FROM "B" TEAM QUARTERBACK TO STARTER

When Drew first arrived on the Westlake High School campus as a skinny young man, not many would have thought he would end his time there with a legendary Texas high school football season and a mantel full of trophies.

After attending the private St. Andrew's Episcopal School for middle school, Drew had changed to a public school for high school. None of the Westlake coaches knew how he could play, putting him at a disadvantage when it came to the football team. Drew had also not played tackle ball yet, since St. Andrew's only participated in the flag leagues. He was practically an unknown entity to the high school coaches, and they already had the varsity team quarterback's younger brother as their "A" team quarterback, so Drew was relegated to the freshman "B" team.

Drew knew he was buried on the depth chart and

was worried he'd never get his chance to play. Even though he led the freshman "B" team to an undefeated season, the next year he would be the second quarterback on the junior varsity squad, behind another student named Jonny Rodgers. Drew was also very good at baseball, so he considered focusing on the other sport and quitting football. He preferred to be on the field rather than sitting on the bench—even if it meant switching from the football field to the baseball diamond.

"I said, 'Mom, I don't think I'm ever going to get a chance to play football, because Jonny's the stud and I'll never beat him out,'" Drew said.

Mina Brees convinced Drew to give it more time, and Drew stayed on the team. During the final preseason scrimmage against the Killeen High School Kangaroos, the summer before his sophomore year, Jonny Rodgers tore a ligament in his knee and couldn't play for the rest of the season. No one was happy that Jonny was injured, but there was still the upcoming football season to think of. Drew was forced into action during the first regular season junior varsity game. He went nine for ten for 315 yards and four touchdowns in that first game as a starter. Drew went on to lead the JV team to an undefeated season.

Drew was playing so well that Jonny knew it would be best for the team if he found a new position and Drew remained the quarterback. Jonny would move to safety and lead the defensive unit while Drew ran the offense. Before his junior year, Drew was named the starter for the varsity team.

With Drew at the helm, the Westlake Chaparrals started winning—and they just kept on winning. After another undefeated season for Drew, his varsity team was playoff bound. The Chaparrals squeaked by San Antonio Madison High School 26–23 before tying San Antonio Marshall 15–15 with a last-second field goal in the first two rounds of the playoffs. Westlake advanced through to the next playoff round on a tiebreaker.

In the third round of the playoffs, Westlake faced Alice High School, a 9–4 team that had lost to Westlake the previous year in the regional semifinals. The game looked like it could spell the end of the Chaparrals' season when Westlake committed three turnovers, including a rare interception of a throw from Brees. All seemed truly lost when Drew went down with a devastating knee injury in the second quarter, and Westlake went into the locker rooms with a ten-point deficit at halftime. Fortunately, Westlake still had star running back Ryan Nunez, and he carried the team. Nunez racked up 205 yards and three touchdowns in the second half to lead Westlake past Alice 42–20. Drew returned to the sideline on crutches to support his team, having torn his right ACL, an important knee ligament. However, with a year still left in high school, Drew's injury was bad enough to put his football career in serious jeopardy.

Without their starting quarterback to lead them, Westlake lost to eventual state champions San Antonio Roosevelt 28–14 in the next round of the playoffs. The Chaparrals' season was over, but as a varsity starter, Drew Brees ended his season with a 12–0–1 record—and was still undefeated.

CHAPTER FOUR
1996

THE COMEBACK KID

Drew's knee injury required surgery, and he was stuck on crutches for months before he could even start rehab. He had to do some serious soul-searching during the off-season between his junior and senior years.

"I had seen a lot of my friends tear their ACLs, and some of them hadn't come back as good as they were before—not as fast, not as mobile, whatever it might be," said Drew. "So the thought of a torn ACL was devastating to me, because I thought that I might be in the same boat as them."

The first injury in one's sports career, especially a major injury, can really shake an athlete's confidence. All the fears and doubts that athletes try to ignore come flooding in. The realities of one's physical limitations, and the fear of further injury, can understandably keep an athlete's spirit down, and can also drastically affect rehabilitation times.

When athletes are injured, they're forced to see themselves without sports in their lives, and it raises a lot of questions. Luckily for Drew, these questions hit him when he was at church one Sunday morning.

"I was seventeen years old, sitting in church one day with a torn ACL, on crutches, wondering what if football were not here for me or if sports weren't here for me," said Drew. "What's my calling in life? What am I? What's my purpose? What am I here to do? For some reason, it all hit me. [The minister's] call to the congregation was that God was looking for a few good men to carry the torch and to represent the Christian faith. I just remember thinking to myself, *Man, I'd like to be one of those few good men.*"

Drew became a Christian, and his faith was a major motivating factor in his rehab, as well as in every decision he made from that point on. He found Coach Carment Kiara at a local Austin-area high school to help create his knee rehabilitation plan, and once Drew started, he never gave up. When Coach Kiara told him to run hills on the hottest day, he did it. Nothing was too tough, and nothing would crush his resolve.

"He never doubted," Kiara said. "He's a doer."

The injury took its toll on Drew physically, but it also hampered his college recruitment prospects. Since he was still rehabilitating his knee, he wasn't able to bring his A-game to any of the summer camps he attended, nor were these the same camps he would have gone to if he hadn't been injured. A lot of college recruitment happened at these summer camps, and even though Drew had just come off an undefeated season, his injury added to the concerns about his size and ability to do well at the college level.

Barely six feet tall and only 180 pounds, Drew didn't fit the mold of the classic quarterback, and college coaches were worried he couldn't handle the harsh and demanding physical expectations of the next level of football. So with the injury and his size working against him, Drew wasn't getting many calls from recruiters. But he knew he could play at the next level at a big Division I program—he just needed to get the offer.

The summer between a player's junior and senior years is a very important time for recruitment. Often, if a player doesn't attract interest during that time period, an offer will never come. Texas A&M, where Drew's father played basketball, and the University of Texas at Austin, where his uncle played football and his mother and father both went to graduate school, weren't interested, so Chip and Mina decided that Drew should start looking at colleges on the East Coast and in the Midwest. Highlight tapes were sent to the University of North Carolina, Iowa, and other colleges that might be a fit—but Drew was told there was no place for him.

"I think sometimes recruiters do get in this mold mentality," Chip said of the experience. "If you have a boy who's six-four, six-five, a recruiter can never be criticized for taking that kid, even if he doesn't work out, because he fit the mold. But if a coach takes a chance on a kid who doesn't fit the mold, now he's leaving himself open to criticism."

The lack of offers, the injury, and his newfound faith must have sparked something in Drew, because the next season he played his heart out.

CHAPTER FIVE
1996–1997

THE LEGENDARY SEASON

No one knew exactly what to expect from the 1996 Westlake High team. Westlake had been a power-house team throughout the decade, progressing to the quarterfinals in the playoffs—if not farther—every year since 1990. They had made two trips to the state finals, in 1990 and 1994. Drew hoped that his 1996 team could make that trip, too, but his knee surgery meant he might not be able to play at a high enough level to lead the team to a state championship game. The team faced another setback, too: many of the previous year's best players had been seniors and had graduated, including running back Ryan Nunez, who was now playing at the University of Colorado. Ryan's departure, in particular, left a big hole in the starting lineup, and no one was sure who was going to be the new running back. There was a lot of uncertainty, and many question marks that year.

Drew was one of only two of the previous year's starters on offense to return for a new season. The other was Drew's co-captain, offensive lineman Seth McKinney. Four of the offensive line that year were brand-new, which meant that the players would need to learn how to work as a team for the first time. On the other side of the ball, Jonny Rodgers, the player Brees took over for as junior varsity quarterback years earlier, returned to ball hawk and lead the defense.

Early in the season, the Chaps won their first game by fourteen points and the next by twenty-three points. Brett Robin, only a sophomore, emerged as the starting running back for Westlake with fullbacks Jamie Tyler and Matt Murphy also getting carries. Drew and the Chaparral offense really got rolling by the third game. They scored over forty points in their third, fourth, fifth, sixth, and seventh games, and won each of those games by double digits. Game after game after game, the team kept winning. By the end of the season, the Westlake Chaparrals were undefeated.

Randy Rodgers, Jonny's father, was in charge of recruiting at the University of Texas. He attended all of the Westlake games and later recalled, "As

Drew got more and more healthy, he just got better and better that year. I remember sitting in the stands about week six or seven and saying, 'This guy is awesome.'"

The buzz around Drew increased throughout the season. His control of the offense was evident to everyone who watched him play. He went through his progressions and checked down on each receiver. He had even shown that he could run with the football. His most impressive skill was an innate ability to slide in the pocket to avoid pressure. He was simply that good, but Drew still didn't get the credit he deserved.

After posting shutouts over the last two games of the regular season, Westlake ran into their first real challenge during the initial round of the playoffs against San Antonio MacArthur. Drew did not have his best game, completing only ten of nineteen passes for 193 yards, but he still tallied two touchdowns in the game, breaking the school record for passing yards in a season. Five of those passes were caught by Drew's favorite target, Ryan Read, whose total of sixty-five catches on the year for 1,221 yards made him the state's top receiver at that point in the season.

That was the closest of the playoff games for the Westlake Chaps. Drew and the rest of the team crushed their playoff opponents, beating San Antonio Clark by fourteen points in the second round, and beating Victoria Memorial by forty-one points in a shutout third-round performance.

In the quarterfinal game, San Antonio Churchill gave Westlake a run for their money, as Churchill scored more against the Chaparrals than any other opponent had that season: twenty-three points. But the Chaps put up forty-nine points to handily win the game. Drew was nineteen of twenty-nine for 344 yards and three touchdowns, two thrown to Read, a 61-yard touchdown and a 30-yard touchdown. Westlake breezed through their semifinal matchup with Aldine High School. Running back Brett Robin ran in two touchdowns, while Drew passed for 246 yards and two touchdowns to cap a 42–23 victory.

Westlake had won fifteen straight games since their quarterfinal loss to San Antonio Roosevelt during the 1995 postseason. Drew had not only made an amazing comeback from his torn ligament, but he had just brought the team to the brink of the state championship and had gone undefeated in the process.

In late December 1996 at Texas Stadium in Irving, the Westlake High School Chaparrals from Austin took the field to face the Oscar Henry Cooper High School Cougars from Abilene. Abilene Cooper were the clear underdogs in this game, but they had come with a game plan. The Cougars were convinced that the key was to neutralize the passing attack. To do that, they had to shut down Drew Brees and force Westlake to run the ball—so the Cougars dropped their linebackers into coverage and blitzed Drew every chance they got.

The game started slowly. It was a slogging defensive battle, and the momentum seemed to turn against Westlake when Cooper's running back Dominic Rhodes gave the Cougars a 7–0 lead in the second quarter. Things got worse for Westlake when Brett Robin, the Chaps leading rusher, went down in the second quarter with a knee injury and could not return to the game. Drew did not complete a pass in the first quarter, and Westlake only managed 133 total yards of offense, going into the half with the game tied 7–7. Westlake coach Ron

Schroeder needed to change his whole approach. He looked to running back Jamie Tyler, tackle Seth McKinney, and the rest of the offensive linemen to carry the load.

Safety Aaron Santiso opened the second half by returning an interception, one of eight forced turnovers for the game, deep into Cougar territory. During Westlake's first offensive series, the Chaps abandoned their pass and gave the ball to Tyler, who pounded it down to the one-yard line, where Coach Schroeder ran Drew on a quarterback sneak to put Westlake ahead by seven.

After this, Westlake never gave up the lead. The defense held Cooper and forced them to punt. Then Tyler ran for a twenty-three-yard touchdown for a fourteen-point lead. Cooper then fumbled the ensuing kickoff and defensive back Tomi Keah jumped on the ball two yards from the goal line. Moments later, Drew tallied another rushing touchdown on his second quarterback sneak of the day. At just over ten minutes into the third quarter, Westlake had built a twenty-one-point lead by forcing a few turnovers and some effective running.

Once Westlake had a lead to play with, they unleashed Drew's aerial attack. In the fourth quarter, Brees hit Jeremy Amos for a forty-seven-yard touchdown pass and then added a twenty-yard touchdown to Matt Murphy for a thirty-five-point lead midway through the fourth quarter. In the second half, the Chaps had scored forty-eight points for a total of fifty-five—more than they had scored all year—and had only allowed Abilene Cooper to score eight. After the dust settled, Westlake had turned a tight game into a blowout 55–15 victory to win the Class 5A Division II state championship game.

It was a magical season, one that has become legendary in Texas high school football lore. Westlake remained undefeated and was ranked at number eight nationally by the *USA Today* National High School Football Rankings. Drew had passed for 3,528 yards and thirty-one touchdowns, breaking both school records, and had thrown only ten interceptions. In fact, during the 1996 season, he broke the records for individual offense during a single game with 364 total yards, individual offense for the season with 3,656 total yards, career individual offense with 5,714 total yards, and career touchdowns with fifty.

That 1996 Westlake championship team left their

mark all over the school's record books, breaking over twenty records that year. Wide receiver Ryan Read teamed up with Drew to set a single-season state record for receptions with 108.

Drew ended his amazing high school career undefeated as a starter, finishing with a 28–0–1 record and having completed 211 of 333 passes for a 63 percent completion rate. In recognition of their achievements, Read, Brees, and McKinney were named to the 5A All-State team. For his remarkable season, Drew was named 5A Offensive Player of the Year and All-Centex Offensive Player of the Year.

It was a perfect season, and you would have expected every scout in the nation to come knocking on the Brees family's door. But they didn't.

CHAPTER SIX
1997–1998

PURDUE UNIVERSITY BOILERMAKERS

For all that he accomplished, Drew did not let the awards and attention go to his head. His Christian faith and the values his grandfather Ray had instilled in him kept him grounded. His coaches noted how respectful he was of adults and referred to him as a "good kid," in praise of his character.

Anyone would say Drew had been a good young man in high school, and he had just ended a storybook season that earned him more trophies than could fit on his mantel—so why hadn't he gotten any calls from recruiters?

"Believe me, we told them he was the most accurate passer we'd ever seen, that he was a great leader and a tough kid," the Chaps offensive coordinator Neal LaHue remembered. "Nobody listened."

Throughout the season, Mina and Chip kept calling schools and sending highlight tapes to drum up interest and help their son's college playing prospects. Nothing. Was it the knee injury? Or his size? Or maybe it was the fact that the University of Texas at Austin had passed on him. Drew was from Austin, and when the school in his own backyard wouldn't even recruit him—the school that had had the most opportunity to scout him—it suggested there was something wrong, something that the other scouts couldn't pick up on from watching Drew in just one or two games. It was a mark against him. According to Drew, Texas A&M had scouted him just long enough to get his hopes up, but that was it.

"I probably wouldn't have recruited myself, either," Drew later said of the experience. "A six-foot quarterback coming off a knee injury—not impressive physical traits, necessarily."

The only offers he got were from the University of Kentucky, which already had a star starting quarterback in future NFLer and Heisman Trophy finalist Tim Couch, and from Purdue University's coach Joe Tiller. Purdue's program hadn't had a lot of recent success, which made Drew a bit hesitant to join its ranks. However, he had always had a sense of where he needed to be and when he needed to be there. He had waited in the wings for his chance to start as quarterback on the junior varsity team when Jonny had gotten hurt, and he'd won the starting job on varsity by being patient, as well. Drew had always proved his doubters wrong when he was on the field. He would let his play do the talking for him, and he knew he'd have a better chance to play at Purdue, since he would have been stuck behind Couch on the bench in Kentucky.

Another deciding factor was Tiller's promise to install the spread offense and an intelligent passing attack geared toward Drew's strengths to help Purdue compete in the storied Big Ten Conference. Despite its lack of recent success, Purdue University was known as the Cradle of Quarterbacks, and had been home to the likes of Super Bowl–winning quarterbacks Len Dawson and Bob Griese. Drew decided he was determined to leave his mark on the school as well.

"Fate, destiny, whatever you call it," Drew's father, Chip Brees, said, "he ended up at exactly the right place for him at exactly the right time."

The move from high school to college can be a difficult transition for everyone, athletes included. Some athletes relish the newfound freedom of the college experience, while others flounder with the lack of structure. The expectations are simply higher—in the classroom and on the field—and many student athletes struggle to adjust that first year. Many young college football players talk about the change in the speed of play. It can be overwhelming, especially for freshman quarterbacks, which is part of the reason that so many of them spend their first seasons on the bench, learning the game.

Drew Brees was talked about as the new stud quarterback when he arrived on campus in West Lafayette, Indiana, and the fans were excited to see what he could do. The Purdue University Boilermakers football team had not been successful for quite some time. In fact, they hadn't had a winning season in over a decade, and Coach Tiller had been hired to revive their fortunes. Tiller knew that he had found some gems in his last recruiting class, including the skinny kid from Austin, Texas, who always found a way to win, but the coach also knew he had to be patient. He would waste Drew's talent if he started him before he was ready.

The 1997 season was quiet for Brees. He spent it on the bench, behind Billy Dicken on the depth chart. He saw infrequent action on game day, mostly in cleanup duty at the end of games. That season was one of learning the playbook and adjusting to college and getting settled in a new state. Drew soaked up every bit of information he could, both in the classroom and on the field. It was a time of growth for the young quarterback.

After sitting his first year, at the beginning of the 1998 season, Drew was ready to start. His first game was against the University of Southern California Trojans. It was the first time Purdue and USC had met since 1976.

The game started well enough for Drew and the Boilermakers, as the quarterback completed five of his first six passes and threw a beautiful touchdown for a seven-point lead. Drew didn't get much time to sit, as he was called back into action after the Trojans returned the ensuing kickoff for a touchdown. He put the Boilermakers up again with a sweet nine-yard strike to wide receiver Cliff Jackson, and Purdue went into halftime up only 17–10 despite posting 208 yards offense to 78 for the Trojans.

USC made a crucial personnel shift at halftime, bringing in the unknown freshman Carson Palmer as quarterback. That one move changed the atmosphere of the game. The Trojans scored seventeen unanswered points to seal a 27–17 win. It was a tough way to lose, but Brees and Palmer received national attention across the country for their solid performances. Drew, in his first start, had completed thirty passes in fifty-two attempts for a 58 percent completion rate and two touchdowns. Coach Tiller also made it known that Purdue was going to play an exciting aerial attacking brand of football. Purdue fans were ecstatic. For the first time in years, there was the potential for greatness on the field.

Purdue beat Rice and Central Florida in non-conference games in West Lafayette before traveling to northern Indiana to face their rival Notre Dame, then ranked twenty-third. In the first quarter, Drew was amazing. He became the leader of his team that game. Hitting his short routes crisply and throwing accurately, he quickly put the Boilermakers up by two touchdowns with a thirteen-yard pass and a two-yard quarterback run. By halftime, Purdue was up 24–14, but that lead dwindled over the second half. Drew couldn't find his rhythm after the break, so he started to force the ball. Purdue managed only two field goals the rest of the game, and Drew threw an untimely interception that let Notre Dame squeak out a win at the last minute. It was another bitter loss, and it taught Drew a good lesson: great quarterbacks control the ball, are consistent, and never lose focus.

"We had the game won. All we had to do was get a first down or punt and let the defense do the rest," Drew said afterward. "We had great confidence in our defense, but I just overthrew the receiver. It was a bad decision on my part, but I knew I could make the throw. I just threw it high. I made a mistake. Next time I have to throw it on the numbers."

The next game, Drew rebounded from his mistakes and unleashed an aerial assault on Minnesota, going thirty-one of thirty-six for 522 yards and throwing six touchdowns—completing passes to ten different receivers—to take down the previously unbeaten Minnesota team 56–21. He threw for 368 yards and four touchdowns in the first half alone. He broke two school records, one for passing yards and the other for the number of touchdowns in a game. His performance also helped the team set school records in total offense of 692 yards, the third highest in Big Ten Conference history. Despite his amazing game, Drew remained the always-humble leader he had been at Westlake, even after earning the nickname Drew "the Hurricane" Brees.

"I just tried to execute our normal offense. I can't really think of any great passes," he said. "The receivers just made all the catches. The offensive line played great and gave me a lot of time."

Brees continued to break records in the next game against number-ten-ranked Wisconsin and future-Heisman-winning running back Ron Dayne. In that game, he tied an NCAA record when he completed fifty-five passes, and broke an NCAA record with eighty-three pass attempts in the game. Unfortunately, he also threw four interceptions, and the Boilermakers lost a close game by seven points.

"Anybody can throw eighty-three times. It's just a matter of completing them and not throwing four interceptions," Drew said after his performance against Wisconsin. "My arm's fine. I could have thrown a hundred more passes. I can't believe we lost the game."

After a loss to number-twelve-ranked Penn State, the Boilermakers were staring at a losing 3–4 record. But then Purdue roared back, winning the last five games of the 1998 season, including a comeback win over Michigan State, and ended the year 9–4 with an invitation to the Alamo Bowl. Along the way, Drew set school records for completions (361), attempts (569), yards (3,983), and touchdowns (39), and was named the Big Ten Offensive Player of the Year.

The Kansas State Wildcats were not happy to be facing the 9–4 Boilermakers in the Alamo Bowl. Kansas State, the fourth-ranked team in the nation, had been in the running for the national title before losing to Texas A&M in the Big 12 Championship game. They were upset about that defeat—they lost by three points in double overtime—and about not getting invited to a more prestigious bowl against a ranked opponent, since they were ranked so highly. The week before the game, all the media coverage was about Kansas State's unhappiness at having to face what they considered a less-than-equal team. They went into the game expecting to crush the unranked Boilermakers, so they were not mentally prepared for a serious fight. Kansas State was overconfident.

The Wildcats were led by quarterback Michael Bishop, who had been their starter for two years. During the 1998 season, he broke numerous school records, was the Heisman runner-up behind Ricky Williams, was named a consensus All-American, and won the Davey O'Brien Award for the best quarterback in NCAA football. It had been a great season for Bishop.

The first quarter started slowly. Kansas State didn't have their heart in the game—the emotional letdown from the season was too much to overcome. Both teams couldn't find the end zone. Drew was the first to score a touchdown early in the second quarter. By halftime, Purdue had held Kansas State to one touchdown and was leading 17–7—but the Kansas State's offense couldn't be counted out of any game.

In the third quarter, Kansas State and Purdue each recovered fumbles in the end zone. The Wildcats had done enough to keep themselves in the game, but they still did not look as dangerous as they had during the regular season. In the fourth quarter, Kansas State University really started to play. First they rushed for a touchdown, then quarterback Bishop threw for two big touchdowns. The resulting twenty-one points allowed the Wildcats to take a 34–30 lead with just over a minute remaining. Purdue fans were crushed. There was no chance for a tie to push the game into overtime—the Boilermakers needed to score a touchdown and win outright. It seemed that the game was over.

With 1:27 left on the clock, Drew and the rest of the Purdue team marched down the field. Drew advanced the ball with an array of passes. When the Wildcats were flagged for a fifteen-yard pass interference, he saw his chance and threw a twenty-four-yard touchdown pass. Purdue had made the impossible possible: in a major upset, they won the game 37–34.

Overall, this had not been Drew's best performance. He was twenty-five of thirty-three for 230 yards and a 47 percent completion rate, well below his 63 percent completion rate for the season. He did throw three touchdowns, but he also threw four interceptions, while he had previously thrown four interceptions all season. Drew's Alamo Bowl performance was not defined by his mistakes, but by his ability to overcome them. Vince Lombardi once said, "It's not whether you get knocked down; it's whether you get up." Luckily for Purdue, Drew had learned that lesson, as he proved during the final, game-winning drive. That day his game and ability seemed to take another step forward. Not bad for a sophomore. But could he continue to build on his success next season?

CHAPTER SEVEN
1999

A DISAPPOINTING YEAR

If 1998 was a great year for Drew, then 1999 was the opposite. The season started out well enough: Drew was named the offensive team captain, and the Boilermakers won their first four games, including a payback win over number-sixteen-ranked Notre Dame. Purdue even peaked in the rankings at number eleven that season. However, the games the Boilermakers were scheduled to play included a stretch of four against nationally ranked teams, including fourth-ranked University of Michigan Wolverines in Ann Arbor. They lost to the Wolverines 38–12 and then to Ohio State in a close match after that.

Purdue always started their games strong behind quarterback Drew's arm, but the Boilermakers lost focus and wilted as the game wore on. It was a pattern that would continue to haunt them all season. They weren't living up to the high expectations of the Purdue fans, who had so happily cheered on their team at the Alamo Bowl.

One of the bright points of the 1999 season was when Purdue, then ranked twentieth, hosted the number-five unbeaten Michigan State Spartans at Ross-Ade Stadium in West Lafayette. At the time, the now-legendary Nick Saban was head coach of Michigan State. He had rebuilt the program during the four years since he took the helm after a disastrous 1994 season, when the Spartans lost all eleven games. Now the Spartans were strong; these were the titans Drew and his team would have to defeat.

Purdue went into the game knowing that small mistakes could cost them the game. They needed not only to start strong, but to stay strong throughout the game. The best way to do that was to give Drew the ball and let him do what he had always done best—throw!

So Drew threw the ball—a lot—to wideout Chris Daniels; those two Boilermakers would go on to make history in that game. Michigan State struck first when Plaxico Burress caught an eighteen-yard touchdown early in the first quarter, putting the Spartans up 6–0. The Purdue team and its fans were worried when the Spartans took the lead. No

one wanted the rival team's offense to start working against the Boilermakers; if they did, Purdue
could lose control of the game quickly. Everyone
was anxious—everyone but Drew.

That day, Drew put on a show for the entire
nation. He threw three touchdowns in the first
quarter alone, putting Purdue up 21–6. By the halftime whistle, he had extended the lead to 35–14 as
he completed twenty-three of thirty-three passes
for 344 yards. He had also thrown three touchdowns to Daniels, who ended the first half with 200
yards, receiving on twelve catches.

In the second half of the game, Michigan State
came out determined to win, and almost immediately put two touchdowns on the board, cutting
Purdue's lead to seven points. That was when Brees
drove the Boilermakers down the field and pulled
a touchdown back with a one-yard run. Michigan
State never scored again. Purdue's defense swarmed
the Spartans during the fourth quarter, closing the
game out with a twelve-yard fumble return for the
last seven points of the game.

When the final whistle sounded, Purdue had
blown out the very good Michigan State with a
score of 52–28. Drew and Daniels had connected

for a Big Ten Conference record twenty-one passes. Drew had thrown for 509 yards. He had completed forty passes in fifty-seven attempts and had scored four touchdowns. But, still, he stayed humble.

"This is probably the biggest win of my career, because people were saying we would lose four straight after losing at Michigan and Ohio State," Brees said. "We were fortunate to get some good weather, and the offense came to play today. The last two weeks, we didn't take advantage of our chances. We did a lot better job of that today."

Purdue split the rest of the season, losing to two top-ten teams in Penn State and Wisconsin, while beating Minnesota and bitter rival Indiana. They ended the season with a 7–5 record overall, a 4–4 record in the Big Ten, ranking twentieth in the nation. It wasn't a bad season, but it also hadn't been the season the Boilermakers had hoped for when they started 4–0.

Still, Purdue had played well enough to get an invite to the Outback Bowl against the number-twenty-one University of Georgia Bulldogs. As was usually the case in many of their games throughout the 1999 season, the Boilermakers offense got off to a great early start. Drew threw three touchdown passes in the first quarter, after which he threw another touchdown to put his team up by twenty-five points before Georgia even had a chance to score. By halftime, however, Purdue had made a few mistakes that allowed Georgia to get back into the game.

It was a tale of two halves as the Bulldogs found a way to block the Boilermakers offense in the second half. Georgia kept Purdue from scoring, while putting up fifteen points to tie the game. In overtime, Georgia kicked a twenty-one-yard field goal to secure the greatest comeback in the history of bowl games.

Even though the loss capped off a disappointing season overall, it was an impressive year for Drew. He'd done well against some of the best competition in the country. He finished with 337 completions out of 554 attempts for 3,909 yards and twenty-five touchdowns. He was a second team All-American and first team All–Big Ten. He received the first-ever Socrates Award, which recognizes an athlete who upheld the highest academic, athletic, and community service standards. He was the runner-up for the Davey O'Brien Award and the Maxwell Award for the nation's top player, and he even finished fourth in the Heisman voting. While his team had not done as well as he'd hoped, Drew Brees had begun to stand out as a top college athlete.

Suzanne Plunkett, AFP Photo/Getty Images

DREW (FAR LEFT) AND THE OTHER FINALISTS BEFORE THE WINNER OF THE 66TH HEISMAN TROPHY WAS ANNOUNCED. FROM LEFT TO RIGHT ARE: DREW BREES OF PURDUE UNIVERSITY; RUNNING BACK LADAINIAN TOMLINSON OF TEXAS CHRISTIAN UNIVERSITY; QUARTERBACK JOSH HEUPEL OF THE UNIVERSITY OF OKLAHOMA; AND THE WINNER, QUARTERBACK CHRIS WEINKE OF FLORIDA STATE UNIVERSITY.

CHAPTER EIGHT
2000

SENIOR YEAR

Drew seriously considered leaving Purdue University to join the NFL during the 1999 season. Because he had been a Heisman Trophy finalist, he was being talked about as a possible high-round draft pick for NFL teams. With his girlfriend set to graduate, and knowing that he could make millions of dollars in the NFL, leaving college for a professional football career was quite a temptation. But was he ready for the jump? Had he learned all he needed to from the Boilermakers? In the end, Drew's sense of commitment and dedication helped him decide to stay.

Drew explained his decision: "There are a lot of things, myself and the team, which are goals that we haven't accomplished," he said. "The main reason is there is a lot of unfinished business. I have a lot of personal goals, but I don't really share them. All I can say is I just want to get better every time I go out on the field."

With Drew returning to school, along with many starters from the previous year, Purdue entered the season ranked fifteenth in the nation. The Boiler-makers won their first two nonconference games against Central Michigan and Kent State in blow-outs. The season was rolling along well—until they ran into one of their biggest rivals.

Brees had split his last two meetings against Notre Dame. And this year the game was in South Bend, Indiana—directly in enemy territory! It was a hard-fought game from the start. The Fighting Irish got into the end zone twice in the first quar-ter. In the second quarter, however, the momen-tum shifted to the Boilermakers, who responded by scoring two touchdowns themselves. At halftime, Purdue was down by only a field goal.

The rest of the game became a defensive bat-tle, with neither team's offense able to score many points. Going into the fourth quarter down six points, Drew found his rhythm. It was as if the game was moving in slow motion for him. He could see his open receivers, and he began to move the ball down the field with ease. He hit wide receiver Vinny Sutherland for Purdue's only score of the second half, a twenty-two-yard touchdown that put the Boilermakers up by one point with just over three minutes left to play. The fans went wild— they thought the Boilermakers had this game in the bag. Unfortunately, three minutes left on the clock ended up being just enough time for Notre Dame. With the clock running out, Fighting Irish kicker Nick Setta made a thirty-eight-yard field goal. Purdue lost 23–21. It was a big disappointment.

On October 7, 2000, Purdue University—now unranked—hosted the sixth-ranked Michigan Wolverines at their home field in West Lafayette. The Wolverines' only loss that season had come at the hands of a very good UCLA Bruins team three weeks earlier. By the time they met Purdue, the Wolverines had already beaten ranked Illinois and Wisconsin teams.

Drew Brees and the Boilermakers played their hearts out—but unfortunately, Drew Henson and the Wolverines were playing well, too. In the second quarter, Michigan scored three touchdowns for a 28–10 lead as time ran out in the first half. Brees would have to find a way to engineer three touchdowns if Purdue wanted to win the game.

Purdue University spent the third quarter scratching their way back into the game. Running back Steve Ennis scored on a one-yard run, but the Boilermakers only came away with six points. As Purdue found some success on the ground, Drew Henson and the Wolverines offense sputtered to a stop. Purdue scored thirteen points, and even though Michigan managed three points in the second half, Drew Brees laid the groundwork for an amazing comeback when he threw a ten-yard touchdown with seven minutes left to play. On the other side of the ball, the Boilermakers defense, led by defensive end Akin Ayodele, continued to force the Wolverines to punt the ball.

"The first half, our defense came out flat, and we weren't ourselves," Ayodele said. "We regrouped, and coach Tiller told us we had to believe. We had to play our own style of defense, and we did."

With just over two minutes left in the game, Brees drove the Wolverines deep into their own territory, but Purdue kicker Travis Dorsch missed a thirty-two-yard field goal that would have given the Boilermakers a one-point lead with their defense playing lights out. Ayodele and the defensive unit walked out onto the field knowing that they had to hold the Wolverines one last time or the game was over. Michigan couldn't manage a single play against that defense and went three and out.

Purdue's offense got the ball back near midfield with 1:41 left on the clock. Brees ran a hurry-up drive (where the team avoids delays between plays) down to the Michigan twenty-one-yard line. As he tried to execute his next play, Michigan was caught with twelve men on the field, pushing Purdue to the sixty-yard line.

With four seconds left in the game, Travis Dorsch kicked a thirty-three-yard field goal just as time expired, giving Purdue a 32–31 victory over the Wolverines. It was the Boilermakers' biggest win of the season.

It had been a great game for Drew. He was accurate the entire time, completing thirty-three for forty-four for 286 yards and a pair of touchdowns. While he'd played technically well, he also proved himself to be a steadfast, unflappable leader. The Heisman hype only grew after that game against Michigan, but Drew didn't pay attention to it. All he wanted was to win games and receive the best bowl game invitation possible—maybe even the Rose Bowl in Pasadena, California.

Purdue won the next two games to set up a tough matchup with a Big Ten powerhouse: number thirteen, Ohio State. During that game, neither team could find any real offensive momentum at the start. Each mustered only a few points, and the score was a paltry 7–3, in favor of Purdue, at the end of the first half.

The first half was a slog, but things got exciting in the second half. Ohio State seemed to take control in the third quarter. Purdue managed an early field goal before the Buckeyes figured out the Boilermakers defense and put up seventeen points in just over ten minutes to take a 20–10 lead.

Before facing Drew Brees, the Buckeyes had been the stingiest defense in the Big Ten. After throwing three interceptions that day, Drew got in the zone in the fourth quarter. He put the Boilermakers up 24–20 when he found freshman John Standeford in the back of the end zone, before hitting Vinny Sutherland on a nineteen-yard touchdown. The Purdue fans went nuts! The atmosphere at Ross-Ade Stadium was electric, especially when the defense stopped Ohio State and Drew got the ball back with only a few minutes left in the game. It looked like he could put the game out of reach—but he threw a bad pass, and Michael Doss of the opposing team jumped on the opportunity. The interception returned Purdue to the two-yard line, but Doss was quickly forced out of bounds by Drew's heads-up, hustle play. He was not going to let Doss score off his mistake! Despite his efforts, Ohio State punched in a touchdown with just two minutes left in the game. Ross-Ade Stadium went silent. The crowd and the Boilermakers were deflated. This game could determine the whole season.

Two minutes is a lot of time in football. Ohio State hadn't run down as much time as they could have with their touchdown. The game was far from over. Drew forgot about the last drive entirely as he stepped into the huddle. He knew he could score in the next two minutes. This was exactly how he wanted the game to end.

"I knew we would get another chance, because if they scored, we were going into the two-minute drill," Drew said. "I stepped into the huddle and told the guys this is the way it is supposed to be."

Two plays: that was all Drew needed to score a touchdown. On that second play, he passed to wide receiver Seth Morales for a sixty-four-yard game-winning touchdown. That pass pushed Drew's total

54

on the day to 455 passing yards on thirty-nine of forty-five attempts. Time ran out, and Purdue University fans stormed the field to celebrate a historic victory for the school.

Winning against Ohio, especially after having thrown four interceptions, was a great high point for Drew and the Boilermakers. However, the week after that, Purdue lost its big game to Michigan State 30–10, in an emotional comedown. That loss put the Boilermakers and the University of Michigan Wolverines into a two-way tie for first heading into the season finale. Purdue had to beat the Hoosiers of Indiana if they wanted to go to the Rose Bowl. Luckily for them, Indiana didn't do as well as anticipated, and the Boilermakers beat the Hoosiers in the last game of the season 41–13. Purdue would head to the Rose Bowl on New Year's Day for the first time since 1967. What an honor!

The Rose Bowl is the game where the champions of the Big Ten and Pacific-12 Conferences meet at the end of each season. It's a big deal to be a part of the history of the Rose Bowl! That season, number-fourteen Purdue was to face the number-four Washington Huskies, whose only loss had come at the hands of the Oregon Ducks. The Huskies led the game after scoring fourteen points in the first quarter. Drew put in a valiant effort, throwing for 275 yards and a pair of touchdowns, but the Boilermakers defense couldn't stop the Huskies when it counted. In many ways, the Boilermakers were no match for their opponents, and they ended up losing a close game 32–24.

A Rose Bowl win would have been a great way to top off what was another great season, and great college career, for the Purdue quarterback, but Drew seemed to be doing just fine even without it. In 2000, he was named the Maxwell Award Recipient for the nation's best player, finished third in the Heisman Trophy voting, was an Academic All-American, and was named the Big Ten Offensive Player of the Year. He was a finalist for the Johnny Unitas Golden Arm Award for the best quarterback in the country, and a finalist for the Davey O'Brien National Quarterback Award.

Brees ended his career at Purdue with his name all over the record books. He was Purdue's and the Big Ten's career leader in passing attempts (1,678), completions (1,026), passing yards (11,792), passing touchdowns (90), and total offense (12,692), and he was the only quarterback with two 500-plus-yard games. He was named Big Ten Player of the Week eight times in his career, and tied with Heisman Trophy winner Ron Dayne for the most Player of the Week awards. He was so loved and respected, the city of West Lafayette named a street after him: Brees Way.

This was quite an impressive showing for a skinny kid from Austin, Texas, whom everyone had always overlooked! By the end of his college career, Drew Brees had caught the eye of sports fans across the nation—and he hadn't even gotten started yet.

CHAPTER NINE
2001

FIRST THE COMBINE, THEN THE DRAFT

The period directly after a football player's senior season should be a calm time to reflect on all that he accomplished during his college career. It *should* be, but it isn't. For most graduating football players with their sights set on a professional sports career, the winter after their final season is stressful. To get to that next level, a player first has to find an agent, then must prepare for the NFL Scouting Combine, a five-day event that puts every potential player through specific drills, strength and intelligence tests, and team interviews with coaches and general managers. Players who have worked their entire college careers to prove themselves on the field have only five days to prove themselves to NFL scouts, executives, and head coaches. If they do not perform well during the Combine, they have a Pro Day to go through similar drills. After that, they might go through private workouts to show their skills. That means players spend a lot of their time practicing for these workouts. At the same time, agents are trying to leverage every detail about each player to get him into a higher draft position. A lot of money is at stake for everyone involved, as is the future of the drafting teams. A bad showing at the Combine can spell disaster for a previously sought-after player, and a great showing can solidify a player's success in the draft.

Drew Brees had been arguably the best quarterback in the nation over his past two seasons, and he deserved to be a first-round draft pick—but just as when he had applied to colleges, his size and height would again be an issue.

Drew went into the Combine with first-round potential. On many NFL teams' draft boards, he was the second-highest-rated quarterback, right behind Michael Vick, the mobile quarterback from Virginia Tech. Although Drew passed about 2,000 yards more than Vick and rushed for only 71 yards less, Vick was considered to be the better prospect because many thought his style of play in college would translate well to the NFL, and most thought he would and should be the first pick in the 2001 draft.

"Michael Vick is a better athlete than I am—that's obvious," Drew said. "But I can get away when I need to. I won't be busting out and running fifty yards downfield, but I don't have to get that far. I just have to get the first down."

Drew went into the Combine with high expectations. When a player arrives at the Combine, his official height and weight measurements are taken. Drew weighed in at a solid 213 pounds, but his height was recorded as six feet. Drew had always thought he was a little taller, so that official recording came as a blow.

During draft season, the slightest mistake, misquote, or incorrect official measurement can drastically affect a player's status. "Draft buzz," "Draft stock," "sleepers," and "boom or bust" are all terms that are thrown around in the weeks before the actual draft. In that respect, the height of a quarterback is a big deal. Even for someone as talented and successful as Drew Brees. The "short quarterback" label is hard to shake, and teams are known to drop players from their draft boards simply because of height. It's a label that every quarterback fears.

Height wasn't Drew's only obstacle. The day he threw the ball did not go well. Some coaches told him to throw at half speed, but he didn't work that way. There was a rhythm to playing quarterback, a rhythm that Drew needed. Eleven of his throws were strong, but the other nine were not. Some throws came out of Drew's hands poorly and were wobbly; others were simply overthrown or not on target. He did not have his timing down with his receivers, and this affected his throws as well. His workout worried NFL executives throughout the league, and his draft stock began to fall. Some pundits started questioning whether he was even a first-round talent at all.

Drew knew he would have to prove himself all over again. Even so, he was still the second-best quarterback in the draft, which was partially because there was a weak quarterback class that year. After his Combine performance, it was more important than ever to do well during his private workout, especially after he chose not to throw during Purdue's Pro Day.

Thankfully, Drew's private workout was much smoother. He was able to throw to two receivers he was comfortable with, and he was allowed to throw at full speed. For every type of throw, Drew shined! Only two balls touched the ground because of him. His passes had pop, his short routes were crisp, and the ball had a nice spiral when in flight. Drew ended the workout throwing some seventy-yard deep balls that dropped right into the hands of receivers. It was an impressive outing.

By the first day of the 2001 NFL draft, the buzz around Drew Brees was that he would go in the late first round, or—at worst—early in the second round. San Diego had the first pick, and all the mock drafts projected them taking Vick. Before they selected him, however, San Diego wanted to make sure Vick would agree to a contract. The Chargers were coming off a one-win season and needed all the help they could get. What San Diego didn't need was a training camp holdout who wouldn't agree to a contract or would create problems in the locker room as they tried to rebuild their team. San Diego had multiple needs at many positions, as a one-win team naturally would, but their biggest need was for a strong quarterback to lead the offense.

Days before the draft, Vick's representatives wouldn't agree on a contract. The Chargers' new general manager John Butler had a decision to make. Should he choose another player with the first pick, or should he try to trade the pick? The choice was made easier for Butler when he started getting calls from multiple teams asking about trading the first pick. In the eyes of most of the league, Michael Vick was a once-in-a-generation talent, and there were many managers who would do whatever it took to get Vick onto their teams. Butler decided on a draft trade and turned that first pick into four picks and a wide receiver.

Many players were chosen and trade deals were made, but Drew Brees was still waiting for his name to be called. Pick after pick, player after player, Drew waited to hear his name. As the end of the first round came to a close, he still had not been drafted—but neither had any other quarterbacks. He was still the best quarterback available, and there were quite a few teams that needed to fill that position.

With the first pick of the second round, San Diego made their decision: Drew Brees would be their quarterback. What a relief! He heard his name called at last. He was especially happy to have been chosen by San Diego, because he had worked out for them before the draft and liked them as an organization. He was also glad to land on a team where he would have a chance to play, rather than on a team looking for a third-string quarterback to sit on their bench just in case the other two quarterbacks got injured.

"I wanted to be with a team that I could have a chance to challenge for a spot," Drew said. "I thought it was a good fit for me."

Luckily for Drew, the 2001 draft class included some of his friends, too. Seventh-round pick Brandon Gorin had been on the Boilermakers. Drew knew LaDainian Tomlinson, whom the Chargers selected with the fifth pick of the first round—part of the exchange for Michael Vick—from playing football in Texas. They had become good friends during high school, and both had imagined playing on the same NFL team when they went pro. Now it was actually going to happen. It was a dream come true for both players. For San Diego, this draft turned the team around and took them to new heights. Once again, Drew was in the right place at the right time. The draft was over, but the work had just begun.

CHAPTER TEN
2001–2002

GOING PRO

Some players, especially those drafted in the first few rounds, are expected to come into an organization and contribute immediately. Drew was fortunate to have NFL veteran Doug Flutie starting in front of him, which allowed him time to adjust to the speed of play in the NFL and to learn the ins and outs of preparing at the professional level.

Flutie had been brought over from Buffalo when general manager John Butler came from the Bills. In 1984, Flutie had been the Heisman Trophy winner and the Davey O'Brien Award winner himself, and he was respected by players and executives across the league. Flutie had been a starter in the NFL and Canadian Football League since being drafted by the Los Angeles Rams in 1985, and had most recently been the starter in Buffalo in 1999. He was a great quarterback with a strong career— and he was almost forty years old, which meant he would be retiring soon. He was also shorter than any other starting quarterback in the league, standing only five feet ten inches. All in all, he was the perfect mentor for Drew.

To mark the shift from college to the pros, Drew decided to change his uniform number. He had always been a huge baseball fan and considered the sport his first love. When he was younger, he'd wanted to be Ted Williams, so he wore the number nine whenever he played baseball. When he joined the Chargers, he decided he would wear the number nine once more.

The 2001 season was quiet for Drew. The Chargers beat Washington, Dallas, and Cincinnati to begin with a 3–0 record. San Diego, however, won only two more games, and ended the season on a nine-game losing streak.

Drew was watching and learning the entire time. He was listening during team meetings—and he always took notes. He even carried a clipboard on the sideline! He played sparingly in mop-up duty at the end of games, completing only fifteen passes that season. He paid attention as Flutie prepared for games, learned how to watch game tapes as a pro, and waited patiently. Drew was the perfect backup that season; he knew that his time would soon come. He dreamed of the day he would start in the NFL.

In 2002, Marty Schottenheimer was hired as the Chargers' new head coach. With a talent like Drew Brees waiting in the wings, there was pressure to start the backup. But a good head coach knows that big decisions can't be made lightly, and Coach Schottenheimer had to be careful not to rush Drew onto the field before he was ready. The coach knew that Drew might need another year to learn the position before playing at a high level—and also that if Flutie had done a good job of mentoring his backup quarterback, Drew would be ready when the time came to play.

The Chargers had not made the playoffs since 1995, one of the longest playoff droughts in the league at the time, and that only added fire to the quarterback controversy that Schottenheimer inherited as he tried to bring success to the Chargers.

San Diego had spent the off-season fortifying their fast, hard-hitting defense. Schottenheimer knew that his defense could keep the games tight, and that would allow him to take more risks on the offensive side of the ball. This meant he might be able to play the unknown entity—but it was a big risk, and no one knew how the season would play out.

"I feel that, being twenty-three years old with only one year in this league, I'm only going to get better," Drew said. "With each snap, I feel like I'm going to get better. I expect nothing less of myself."

When Drew Brees beat out Doug Flutie for the starting spot, he was the fourth quarterback in the last four seasons to start the season for the Chargers. If he was successful on the field, Drew could provide some consistency at the most important position. To do that, though, he was going to need the help of the man he was replacing. Some were concerned that Flutie would be angry that he was relegated to backup and would fight to regain his starting position, but Flutie was completely professional. He gracefully stepped aside, letting the sophomore quarterback take the helm.

"The only way I have any impact at all right now is through Drew," the elder quarterback Flutie said. "To be able to help and see something I saw transition into a first down or transition into a completion makes me feel good. It makes me feel like a coach more than a player right now. Not that Drew needs a lot of that."

Drew left a mark in his first NFL start. Against the Cincinnati Bengals, he put on a veteran performance, completing fifteen of nineteen passes for 160 yards, as well as a pair of touchdowns. Running back LaDainian Tomlinson did his share, too, rushing for 114 yards, adding another 45 through the air, and scoring a touchdown. The win was especially exciting since the Bengals had a top-ranked defense, and the Chargers managed to score an impressive thirty-four points against them.

Drew repaid Schottenheimer's trust with one solid performance after another, and the Chargers won their first four games of the season. After a disappointing outing against the Broncos, where Drew was intercepted twice on key plays, he led the Chargers to a close win against their division rivals, the Kansas City Chiefs. San Diego's offense found a way to overcome five turnovers that day, while Drew threw two late touchdowns to help the Chargers score twenty-one points in the fourth quarter.

The Chargers went into their bye week with a 6–1 record, first place in the American Football

Mark Leffingwell, AFP Photo/Getty Images

DREW NARROWLY ESCAPES A SACK IN A GAME AGAINST THE
DENVER BRONCOS.

Conference's Western Division (AFC West). The
Chargers were in a great position to take command
of their division and earn a playoff spot, but they
lost their momentum during their bye week off, and
would only win two more games that season. They
finished the season with an 8–8 record and missed
the playoffs.

While Drew had started the season well, he
showed his age at times, making rookie mistakes
and getting caught up in the game. He tried to force
plays instead of letting the plays come to him, as

many more veteran players knew to do. He also had a habit of holding on to the ball too long, not trusting himself enough to find the open receiver.

On the bright side, however, his completion rate was over 60 percent, and he showed good accuracy—though he knew he would have to cut down on the interceptions if he was going to be successful. The Chargers had relied on a strong running game behind the tremendous play of Tomlinson that season, but for the Chargers to start winning, they needed a balanced offensive attack. Drew would need to show some real growth during the off-season before his coach would trust him to win games with his arm alone.

CHAPTER ELEVEN
2003

A DOWN YEAR

During the summer of 2002, John Butler, the general manager who had drafted Drew Brees, was diagnosed with cancer. The Chargers released a statement saying that, "[Butler] is tending to business as usual and wants everyone in the Chargers family to do the same. While he is grateful for the kind thoughts and interest, he wants the entire organization to remain focused on bringing a world championship to San Diego."

When he was diagnosed, Butler met with Dean Spanos, the Chargers' president, to discuss who would take over as the general manager. During that meeting, it was decided that the Chargers had the perfect candidate in-house. Butler had worked alongside A.J. Smith for years in Buffalo and San Diego, and Smith had been Butler's right-hand man. Butler was sure Smith was ready to run the team, and he easily convinced Spanos of the same.

By January 2003, Butler's cancer had gone into remission, and it looked like the plan wouldn't be necessary. San Diego began to prepare for the draft with Butler in charge. But just a month later, he started feeling sick again and his health took a turn for the worse. In April 2003, John Butler died at the age of fifty-six. It was a sad time for the team.

Eleven days later, A.J. Smith took over as the new general manager of the San Diego Chargers. With a new general manager in place, the philosophy of any team can change. Coaches and players can fall out of favor or be traded or released. A change of this magnitude can create a lot of tension within an organization—especially when the team isn't winning.

The year before Drew was drafted, San Diego had won only one game. The two seasons after, the Chargers saw their win totals increase to five and then eight wins. While it wasn't good enough to get the team to the playoffs, eight wins was certainly a big improvement. Unfortunately, that upward trend did not continue during Drew's second year as a starter.

The 2003 season did not go the way the team wanted it to, and both the Chargers and Drew slumped out of the gate. They lost their first five games, and the Chargers went into their break with team morale at an all-time low. Critics singled out Drew Brees as a source of the problem, saying he needed to be more consistent with his play and cut down on turnovers. Others questioned whether he was ready or even capable of playing in the NFL. When the team went down, he tried to do too much—and because of that, he made more mistakes. The more mistakes he made, the more he pressed. It was a cycle that Drew got caught up in over the course of that season.

Drew's up-and-down play continued after the break. As the season wore on, Coach Schottenheimer stopped calling pass plays for the sputtering air attack and relied on his running back, Tomlinson. A poor week-eight performance against the Miami Dolphins that included three interceptions forced Schottenheimer to revisit the idea of playing backup Doug Flutie in week nine against Chicago. Flutie started that game, but Drew was put in for the fourth quarter with the game all but lost, and he helped the Chargers score their only points against the Bears.

Flutie started the next five games, and won two.

With a 3–10 record, the Chargers' season was effectively over, so Schottenheimer chose to start Drew again in the last three games. This decision was more about giving the front office a chance to evaluate Drew and to see how he would react to being benched before the off-season. He played well in two of the games, but could only manage one win. The Chargers finished with an awful 4–12 record on the year. After such a rough season, Drew's future with the team was in serious doubt.

CHAPTER TWELVE
2004

QUARTERBACK CONTROVERSY

With the worst record in the NFL, the San Diego Chargers went into the off-season holding the first pick in the 2004 draft. Speculation about whether they would draft a quarterback was rampant. Eli Manning, Philip Rivers, and Ben Roethlisberger were all considered first-round talents that year. Manning came into the draft with the most buzz, as a huge talent and the younger brother of the amazing Indianapolis Colts quarterback Peyton Manning. He was considered a franchise quarterback, and Drew hadn't played well enough in his short career to convince the Chargers not to draft the younger Manning.

The Chargers loved what Manning could do, and the team was all set to draft him. Eli and Peyton's father, former New Orleans Saints quarterback Archie Manning, traveled to San Diego just days before the draft to meet with the Chargers.

Afterward, however, Eli's agent made it clear that Eli was not interested in playing for San Diego. Obviously something had happened in that meeting. Some in the media speculated that it was a money issue, while others believed that the Manning family wanted to have Eli play in New York. Whatever the reason, the Mannings made it clear that Eli would never play for San Diego.

Coach Schottenheimer had fallen in love with Philip Rivers's playing style during his time coaching the South team in the Senior Bowl. The North Carolina State quarterback was big, standing six feet five inches and weighing 230 pounds, and he could throw the ball with incredible power.

On the day of the draft, San Diego tried to trade their pick, but couldn't find a deal that was suitable. If they were going to give up the first pick in an extremely deep draft, they wanted to get multiple high draft picks in return. New York reached out to San Diego about the pick, but didn't want to give up the right combination of picks or players.

With no real deal on the table, San Diego called the Mannings' bluff, deciding to take the top player on their draft board. With the first pick in the 2004 NFL Draft, the San Diego Chargers selected Eli

Manning from Ole Miss. The Raiders took Robert Gallery with the second pick, and with the third pick, Arizona selected Larry Fitzgerald. With the Giants up next and Gallery off the board, New York waited until time had almost run out on the clock, and then they selected Philip Rivers. Had all the controversy leading up to the draft blown over? Was San Diego really going to risk a holdout by Eli or worse?

Minutes later, a trade was announced. Manning was headed to New York after all, and San Diego would receive Philip Rivers, as well as the Giants' 2004 third-round pick and their 2005 first- and fifth-round picks. It was another great draft day trade for San Diego, but what did it mean for Drew Brees?

Going into the 2004 season, Drew Brees knew he would have some real competition from rookie quarterback Phillip Rivers. He also knew that neither the current coach nor the current general manager had chosen to draft him, and they had just drafted their quarterback in the first round. It was clear to Drew that the San Diego front office wasn't convinced he could play quarterback. But Drew had been in similar situations before—in both high school and college—and he had always proved the doubters wrong.

As training camp started, San Diego and Philip Rivers were stuck in a long contract negotiation that kept the talented rookie out of almost all his first sessions. Rivers's absence allowed Drew to get all the first-team gameplay, putting him in a position where he could prove himself once more. The longer Rivers was a camp holdout, the more time Drew got to practice with his receivers. When Rivers finally reported to training camp in late August, he'd joined the team too late—there was no possibility of the rookie starting in the first game.

Drew would remain the starter for that season. Though he could not have known it then, he would have a brilliant career year, and would even be voted to the Pro Bowl. What a way to welcome the rookie quarterback—and to further the quarterback controversy in San Diego.

The first game of the 2004 season showed San Diego and the Chargers what consistent, smart playing from Drew could do for the team. Drew turned in a great performance, especially when the game was on the line. With the score tied deep in the fourth quarter, Drew completed five big passes, including a nineteen-yard touchdown that led the Chargers to a 27–20 victory over the Houston Texans. He went seventeen of twenty-four attempts and threw a pair of touchdowns. Drew was clean and efficient that day, regaining some of the respect he had lost from his teammates and San Diego's fans. But the most exciting thing about that game might have been watching the play between Drew and tight end Antonio Gates.

Gates was an undrafted free agent who had signed on with San Diego after the 2003 draft. He had been a basketball player in college and hadn't played football since high school, but he'd received more attention from the NFL than the NBA, and so decided it was best to sign with the Chargers. Antonio was great in both the offensive lineman and wide receiver roles, making him a fantastic tight end. He had started the 2003 season as third-string, but he had worked his way up to a starting position by the middle of November. During the off-season, Drew and Antonio had developed a good, friendly relationship, and their trust in each other was making a difference on the field. In that first game against the Texans, Drew threw eight passes to Antonio for 123 yards. A job well done!

Drew's next performance against the New York Jets saw him repeat old mistakes by committing turnovers and trying to force the ball. Clearly frustrated with Drew's performance, Coach Schottenheimer benched Drew for the entire fourth quarter. This made Drew angry, and as he walked off the field, he threw his helmet before getting into a sideline argument with Schottenheimer on camera.

No one was happy, and it started to look like the Chargers were going to implode again, especially when they lost to the Broncos in the third week, in part due to another poor performance by Drew.

In a week-four matchup with the Tennessee Titans, however, something clicked for Drew. He stopped trying to make plays and just threw the ball. He kept it simple, captaining his offense while putting together a complete performance. The Chargers took control of the game in the first quarter and never gave up the lead. Drew threw for 206 yards that day, with only four incomplete passes. He played his best game in some time, and Tomlinson matched that effort, running for 146 yards on seventeen carries. San Diego's steady offense walloped the Titans 38–17. They had found their balanced attack. That game was the start of a historic Chargers run.

By their week-ten bye, San Diego had won five of the last six games and sported a 6–3 record with a three-game winning streak. Their only defeat in their last six games had been a one-point loss to Atlanta and Michael Vick—the quarterback San Diego had almost drafted.

San Diego went on to defeat Oakland, then pulled out close wins against Kansas City, Denver, and Tampa Bay, before blanking the Browns in Cleveland. San Diego had won eight straight games behind the great play of Brees, Tomlinson, and Gates. With these incredible players at the top of their game, the San Diego Chargers cinched their first playoff berth in almost ten years.

In week sixteen, Drew and the Chargers rolled into Indianapolis to take on Peyton Manning and the Colts. While both quarterbacks were doing well, Manning was having one of the greatest seasons in the history of professional football and was two touchdowns away from breaking the single-season record for touchdowns. He was certainly a worthy opponent for Drew Brees!

Drew started the game strong, putting the Chargers up early with a pair of touchdown passes. Leading his team with the new clarity and focus he had discovered, he kept them up by two scores until late in the second half. Unfortunately, the Colts came roaring back toward the end of the game, when Manning helped mount a fifteen-point comeback to win in overtime. Manning's two touchdowns gave him a season total of forty-nine touchdowns and sole possession of the single-season record, but Brees had tossed three touchdowns and gone twenty-one of thirty-one for 290 yards. The two titan quarterbacks had gone toe-to-toe, and in the end, Peyton Manning barely got the better of Drew Brees. Even though Manning had won this time, Drew had made it clear that he could play with the best in the world—and hold his own.

Coach Schottenheimer was impressed with Drew's new show of his abilities, but thought it was best to bench him for the last game of the regular season so he could rest up for the playoffs. Rookie Philip Rivers and veteran Doug Flutie shared quarterbacking duties that game, and the Chargers beat the Chiefs to end the season with a 12–4 record. This fantastic tally came only a year after posting a league worst 4–12 record—it was an incredible feat that the

Chargers had come such a long way in such a short amount of time.

In 2004, the Chargers' record was good enough to put them in first place in the AFC West, which meant they would host the fifth-seed New York Jets during the wild-card round of the playoffs. The Jets had beaten the Chargers earlier in the season, and the Chargers wanted to show that they could win this rematch—and move on to the next round of the playoffs.

In the first quarter, neither team could get an offense going, and by halftime, they were tied 7–7. In the third quarter, Jets quarterback Chad Pennington threw a touchdown, and the Jets kicked a field goal to take the lead with a 17–7 score. In the fourth quarter, San Diego fought back. After a field goal, Brees, Tomlinson, and Gates worked together to drive the Chargers down to the one-yard line. Incredible!

At the one-yard line, Brees found Gates in the back of the end zone on a crossing route to tie the game and send it into overtime. It seemed like the Chargers were heading toward a comeback, but rookie kicker Nate Kaeding missed a field goal that would have won the game. The Jets pounced on that mistake and hit a twenty-eight-yard field goal with just eight seconds left on the clock.

To end the season without advancing in the playoffs was devastating to both the Chargers and to Drew. Despite this, however, Drew had posted career highs in almost every category and had been named the NFL Comeback Player of the Year. His numbers were great: he had completed 65.5 percent of his passes for 3,159 yards, twenty-seven touchdowns, and only seven interceptions. Just one year before, the Chargers had been wondering if they had made a mistake in recruiting Drew—now he was coming into his own as a pro.

CHAPTER THIRTEEN
2005–2006

GOOD-BYE, SAN DIEGO

The 2005 season was a mixed bag. Drew was in the last season of his rookie contract, so he was playing for his job. He didn't play poorly, but at the same time, he didn't take the next steps the franchise was hoping for. Because San Diego had a great rookie waiting in the wings, Drew needed to prove that he was worth a new contract even with Philip Rivers already signed and eager for his chance to become the starting quarterback.

San Diego's schedule of games was a lot tougher that season. Four of the first seven games were against teams that had made the playoffs last season, and Drew knew they would be a formidable challenge. Though they fought hard—and defeated one of the playoff teams—the Chargers lost four of those first games. Each defeat was a very close call, with the Chargers losing by four or fewer points. But in the NFL, a close loss is still a loss, and

Drew and the Chargers would have to win more games if they wanted another chance at the playoffs.

After losing 20–17 to the Philadelphia Eagles, the Chargers won five straight games. San Diego fans began to hope that they would make two straight playoff appearances. Drew threw for 3,576 yards that season, which was the most since Dan Fouts had played for the Chargers—an impressive feat! But even with this strong showing, a playoff appearance was not meant to be. San Diego lost three of their last four games to end the season at 9–7, short of the playoffs. To make matters worse, Drew tore the labrum in his throwing shoulder during the last game—a game he shouldn't even have been playing, since without the playoffs at stake, Philip Rivers should have been given some playing time.

That off-season was a choppy one for Drew. He was out of contract with the Chargers, and he needed shoulder surgery, which hurt his leverage when negotiating a new contract. It would take a leap of faith from the Chargers to sign Drew to a long-term commitment. Many expected the team to place a franchise tag—a one-year commitment to the Chargers, after which he would become a free agent—on him, but instead he was offered an incentive-heavy contract thought to be worth a possible $50 million over five years.

This was certainly a lot of money, but many quarterbacks in the NFL received contracts worth much more, and Drew thought he was a good enough player that he deserved more, too. He had earned a Pro Bowl nod for his play in 2005, and his quarterback rating over the past two seasons was the fifth best in the league. Though his performance was sometimes uneven, Drew had done a lot for the Chargers, including leading them to a playoff game.

"Obviously, going back to this off-season, and even last season, I set out with a goal and a purpose in mind," Brees said. "That was, first of all, to lead this team to a championship. Along with that, to try to become one of the best quarterbacks in this league, although neither of those goals have been accomplished. But that's the path, that's what I strive for."

Despite his play on the field, however, questions about Drew's abilities and his height came up once again. The Chargers were also worried about his torn labrum, and whether, after his surgery, he'd be able to make the kind of impressive game-winning throws the team needed.

When the negotiations started breaking down,

Drew began to get offers from other teams. The New Orleans Saints, the Oakland Raiders, and the Miami Dolphins all expressed interest in him. The Dolphins were coached by Nick Saban, who had been very successful in the college ranks and was now in his second season as a head coach in the NFL. The Dolphins were considering two different quarterbacks: Drew Brees and Daunte Culpepper. Coincidentally, both athletes were healing from injuries. Luckily for Drew, he was the Dolphins' first choice.

Midway through the off-season, rumors that Drew had made a deal with Miami surfaced in the media. He'd been seen arriving in Florida to complete a medical exam, the last step in the contract proceedings. It seemed that he was days away from becoming Miami's new star quarterback. But when the Dolphins doctors examined Drew's shoulder, they decided they'd found too much damage, which scared the organization.

"I was told by some doctors that I had a twenty-five percent chance of coming back and ever playing," Drew said.

If the Dolphins were scared, imagine how Drew must have felt—he'd fought so hard to become a starting quarterback, and his dreams of continuing his NFL career would be dashed without a fully functioning shoulder. To be told that he had a 75 percent chance of never being able to play at the level he'd achieved was devastating. Upon receiving the report, the Dolphins retracted their contract offer and began renegotiating with Drew and his agent, Tom Condon, for less money. Despite fears surrounding his shoulder, Drew was confident he could continue to play. He and Condon decided to look elsewhere.

"We thought Drew Brees was an outstanding player, and that's who we made the first offer to," Saban said. "Quite frankly, you know, he didn't pass the physical with our organization, so we had to go in another direction, and there was nothing any of us could do about that."

Tom Condon had also been in communication with the New Orleans Saints. The Saints loved how Drew threw the ball, and they jumped at the chance to sign him. The whole process happened very quickly. By mid-March, Drew was signed as the Saints starting quarterback with a six-year, $60-million contract thought to have much more favorable terms than the contract San Diego had offered.

Just as important, Drew would be going to a team and city that would really value his play.

"I just felt that energy in New Orleans," Drew said after signing the contract. "From the very beginning, there was a genuine feeling that they wanted me there. They believe I can come back from this shoulder injury and lead them to a championship. They were as confident as I am, and that meant a lot."

Again, Brees had turned something negative into something very positive. He was at the right place at the right time, and it was the beginning of an amazing era for the Saints and for Drew Brees.

CHAPTER FOURTEEN
2006

REBUILDING IN NEW ORLEANS

On August 29, 2005, while Drew was preparing for his last season with San Diego, a Category 3 hurricane called Katrina had made landfall just southeast of New Orleans in the St. Bernard and Plaquemines parishes. Hurricane Katrina brought winds up to 140 miles per hour and was 400 miles wide. The most severe part of the storm never hit the city of New Orleans, but the surge of water that followed caused catastrophic structural failure to the levees surrounding the city, which in turn caused massive flooding in and around the New Orleans metropolitan area.

Almost 80 percent of the city's population had evacuated before the storm, but many of the city's poorer residents didn't have access to a car or other means to escape the rising tides, so Mayor Ray Nagin had designated the downtown Superdome stadium as a last-resort shelter for those unable to leave the city limits. The federal and municipal leaders did not have a comprehensive plan for a disaster of that magnitude.

In the aftermath of the storm, those who were left in the city faced chaos. There was no power, the sewers had flooded, and roads had crumbled. Food and water were scarce. The Superdome failed as a shelter; the conditions were unlivable, unsafe, and unsanitary. Once a symbol of the city's hope, the Superdome had become a symbol of the government's failures in the aftermath of the storm. Hurricane Katrina killed more than two thousand people and displaced approximately four hundred thousand residents. The destruction was massive. In the Ninth Ward and other areas that were at or below sea level, the flooding reached or breached the roofs of the houses and did billions of dollars of damage. The City of New Orleans would never be the same.

During the 2005 season, the New Orleans Saints team understandably wasn't able to play home games in the Superdome. That season the team split their home games between Tiger Stadium, where the Louisiana State University team played, and the Alamodome in San Antonio. The Saints struggled that season and finished with a 3–13 record, the second worst in the league. Head coach Jim Haslett was fired as the Saints looked to rebuild the team with a new coach and a new quarterback, even as New Orleans focused on rebuilding the city itself.

Sean Payton had been an assistant head coach with Dallas for three seasons before being named as the Saints' new head coach in the winter of 2006. Payton's first move was to find himself a new quarterback, and his first choice was Drew Brees. Fans were skeptical of Payton's decision to recruit Drew. The new contract seemed like a lot of money to spend on a short quarterback with an uneven record and an injured shoulder.

Still, Payton followed his instinct and signed Drew. Once he had a quarterback in place, he continued the rebuilding process for the Saints through the NFL draft. In the first round, the Saints took Heisman running back Reggie Bush, and in the second, they selected safety Roman Harper. Both players would become integral parts of the team.

The team went into training camp with the hope that the coming season would be better than their last one. Drew, on the other hand, spent most of the off-season rehabilitating his shoulder. He needed to be ready to play come week one of the season. When he wasn't rehabbing, Drew was helping his family relocate to New Orleans, a city still struggling to recover from the destruction of Hurricane Katrina.

Soon after Drew signed with the Saints, former Pro Bowl and Saints quarterback Archie Manning welcomed him to the city with a phone call. Football fans in Louisiana have always been extremely proud to know that the first family of football, the Mannings, hail from New Orleans—and to have Archie

Chris Graythen/Getty Images

DREW BREES AUTOGRAPHS A FOOTBALL AFTER PRACTICE ON THE FIRST DAY OF TRAINING CAMP FOR THE NEW ORLEANS SAINTS ON JULY 28, 2006.

Manning's blessing meant a lot to Drew and to the fans. The Mannings were so friendly and welcoming, in fact, that they helped the Brees family find their house and gave them advice on restaurants. The friendship grew from there, with Drew even telling reporters that Archie would text him before games to wish Drew and the Saints good luck.

The 2006 season was exactly what the city needed. The Superdome reopened before the first home game, allowing the Saints to once again play in New Orleans. Coach Payton and Drew brought a new energy to the team. After they beat the Cleveland Browns without Drew needing throw a single touchdown, Payton knew he had his man in Drew Brees.

"Don't worry about Drew Brees," Payton said. "He's the player we thought he'd be when we signed him. He's the guy you want out there taking sixty-five snaps a game. He's not the guy who punches the clock on coming to work. He's always working, always thinking, which is what you have to do if you're a quarterback in this league."

New Orleans won five of their first six games, while their new quarterback averaged over 250 yards per game with a 66.4 percent completion, eight touchdowns, and only four interceptions.

After their week-seven bye, the Saints slumped and lost three of four games. They still had a 6–4 record, however—twice as many wins as in their previous season, and they finished the season at 10–6. That made New Orleans fans, also sometimes known as the Who Dat Nation very hapy. "Who dat?" has long been a chant of sports team support, referencing the idea that anyone who thinks they can beat the home team is wrong, and it's been most widely used by the New Orleans Saints, to the point where the phrase has come to be associated fully with the Saints. The attention of the Who Dat fans—and the entire city—was captured by the 2006 season, and Drew's phenomenal play was at the center of the team's success.

New Orleans had gone from worst to first in a single season. They were in first place in the National Football Conference (NFC) South, and that earned them a bye in the opening round of the playoffs. Additionally, the Saints would have home-field advantage in their first postseason game. It had been more than ten years since the Superdome had hosted a playoff game. That year the Saints and their fans turned the reopened Superdome into a fortress, so the home game would be a big advantage for New Orleans.

Even with the home advantage, the Saints would not have an easy time beating the Philadelphia Eagles. The teams were similar in many ways. Both had strong running backs who could make plays and break long runs, and both had stout defenses. The main difference between the teams was their quarterbacks. In many ways, Drew could be considered the superior quarterback. If he played within himself and limited turnovers, he could tilt the game in the Saints' favor.

Deuce McAllister, the Saints' bell cow running back (the running back with the majority of carries), and rookie scat back (the running back most valued for speed and agility) Reggie Bush found their rhythm early in the game. After a pair of field goals, Bush scored the Saints' first touchdown on a four-yard run to put New Orleans up 13–7, but the defense let Brian Westbrook, the Eagles running back, score on the subsequent series. At halftime, the score was 14–13, and it was still anyone's game.

The Saints kicked off to the Eagles to start the

second half. On the third play of the series, West-brook made a sixty-two-yard touchdown. Less than two minutes into the third quarter, the Saints were down 21–13. For many teams, a run like that would shift the momentum, and the offense would start to force the ball or try to find a big play of their own—but not these Saints. Five yards here and seven yards there, the Saints offense moved the ball behind McAllister and Bush. Drew came through with great passes, and New Orleans methodically moved the ball to the Eagles' five-yard line, where McAllister punched in a touchdown to pull the Saints within a point.

New Orleans defense made a great stop to force a Philly punt, and the Saints got the ball back on the sixteen-yard line. They drove down the field again, but a Bush fumble almost ended the series. If it had not been for the reaction of wide receiver Terrance Copper, who dropped on the ball to keep the drive alive, they might have lost the game. The Saints would retake the lead when Brees hit McAllister on an eleven-yard out to make the score 27–21 with just a minute left in the third quarter.

That would be the last time New Orleans would score in the game, but the defense stepped up and held the Eagles to a single field goal during the fourth quarter. The Saints won! Next up would be their first-ever NFC championship game.

Things didn't go as well in the NFC Championship. The Chicago Bears ran all over New Orleans as their defense shut down the Saints offense. Drew did his best to keep his team in the game, but four Saints turnovers and twenty-one points from the Bears in the fourth quarter ultimately sank New Orleans.

Despite this, Drew and his teammates had a lot to be proud of. The Saints had made it all the way to the doorstep of a Super Bowl after a terrible season the year before. Coach Payton was named Head Coach of the Year for his work, and Drew Brees was named first-team All-Pro along with tackle Jammal Brown.

Drew's contributions weren't just on the field. His work in the community, and what he gave back to the fans, was even more important than what he'd done for the Saints. He was named the Walter Payton NFL Man of the Year for his charity work and his performance on the field. He ended up sharing the award with his friend and former teammate LaDainian Tomlinson.

"Drew has done a fantastic job here post-Katrina," Archie Manning said. "It was so unique for Drew to come here, the way people latched onto the Saints for an emotional lift after Katrina. But Drew took that ball and ran with it."

The success of the team didn't fix anyone's house or repair the streets, but for a few Sundays during the end of 2006, the Saints helped rebuild the spirits of the people of New Orleans. It gave the fans time to forget their troubles and remember how it felt to have hope again.

CHAPTER FIFTEEN
2007–2008

THERE ARE RECORDS TO BE BROKEN

For every up, there is a down. This is never truer than in sports. After a monumental season like 2006, anything less than perfection the next season was bound to be a letdown. The expectations were quite high for the team to repeat its success, but no one took into consideration the Saints' schedule. Because of their strong record the previous year, they would face a tougher schedule during the 2007 season. They lost four games straight to start the season, proving it would be an uphill battle. They then won four games straight and sat at 4–4, but then only managed to win three of the last eight games. With a 7–9 record, the Saints finished third in the NFC South, and they were well out of the playoff picture.

The 2008 season wasn't much better. They did win one more game to end at .500, but they actually finished at the bottom of their division. Despite the results and the playoff drought, there was still a lot for Saints fans to be happy about: the team's air attack became one of the best in the league, and much of that had to do with Drew. In 2008, he mounted the first of a series of assaults on the record books.

The first of the records Drew approached breaking belonged to Dan Marino, who was considered the best quarterback to have never won a Super Bowl. In fact, he made only one appearance there: Marino led the Miami Dolphins to Super Bowl XIX, but he had the misfortune to play against Joe Montana, arguably the best quarterback to play the game. During that 1984 season, Marino became the first quarterback in the history of the NFL to throw over 5,000 yards in a season when he threw for 5,084 yards. To this day, he still has a dozen active records in the NFL, despite ending his career in 1999.

Drew did his best to challenge Marino's record in 2008. He threw for 300 or more yards ten times that season and for over 400 yards twice. By the last game of the season, he was hovering at 4,683 yards—just 402 yards from breaking Marino's record. Drew attempted forty-nine passes and scored four touchdowns in that game, but could only manage 386 yards. While fifteen yards short of the record, he became only the second quarterback to throw for over 5,000 yards. His performance during the 2008 season also won him the Associated Press Offensive Player of the Year, as well as a trip to the Pro Bowl as a first-team All-Pro.

Over his first three seasons with New Orleans, Drew worked as hard as any player out there. He prepared for games, he studied, and he strove tirelessly to get better and to bring wins to Saints fans. As a result, Drew had fashioned himself into an elite pro quarterback and cemented his legacy in the hearts of the Who Dat Nation. Once skeptical, New Orleans now thought of Drew as one of its own. He had brought respect to the Saints, but one thing was still missing: the Super Bowl.

Every season, Drew's singular goal was to win the Super Bowl and bring a world championship to New Orleans. The city deserved it—and the fans deserved it, too. Until he did that, it was time to go back to work. During the 2009 off-season, Drew worked harder than ever. He now had two important jobs: as a quarterback and as a first-time father. Drew's son, Baylen Robert Brees, was born on January 15, 2009, which was also Drew's thirtieth birthday. Now he'd be up all night taking care of his crying son on top of working all day, but that wasn't anything Drew Brees couldn't handle.

CHAPTER SIXTEEN
2009–2010

A CHAMPIONSHIP SEASON

The start of the 2009 season was difficult for Drew because his mother, Mina, died suddenly in August. Drew and Mina had been estranged and hadn't talked very much since he went pro. His mother had at first wanted to be his NFL agent, but Drew didn't like the idea of mixing family and business, so he turned her down, and Mina did not take it well. But their relationship had been improving before she passed away. It was a tough time for Drew, but his faith and family were there to comfort him.

And, of course, there was football. If there were any questions about Drew's focus or commitment, the first game of the 2009 season answered them all. The Detroit Lions never had a chance. Drew had spent the entire off-season working on his release and footwork, and those efforts paid off. Additionally, the Saints had signed Darren Sharper to a one-year contract to help complete their defense. Both the defense and Drew had a great game.

After a good return on the first-half kickoff, Drew attacked the Lions early and put their defense on their heels. In less than three minutes, he moved the Saints into Lions territory and hit wide receiver Marques Colston right below the upright for a nine-yard touchdown. After the defense forced the Lions to go three-and-out, Drew connected with Robert Meachem on a beautiful thirty-nine-yard pass to put the Saints up by two touchdowns.

In the second quarter, Brees decided to spread the ball around a bit more. He found his tight end for two easy touchdowns. Darren Sharper then did what he was brought to New Orleans to do— he picked Lions quarterback Matthew Stafford on the goal line to end the half. The Saints dominated the first half and led 28–10 by the whistle.

When both teams stepped on the field for the second half, however, it looked as though the Saints had lost a bit of their urgency; the offense stalled at the beginning of the third quarter. With just over three minutes left, Drew launched a fifty-eight-yard laser to wide receiver Devery Henderson for an end-zone dance, putting the Saints up by eighteen points.

When Brees and the Saints finally stopped rolling on the Lions, the Saints quarterback had thrown passes to eight different receivers for 358 yards, and had completed twenty-six of thirty-four passes. He averaged over ten yards per completion en route to a 45–27 burner. Plus, he hadn't been sacked once, a testament to his speed and the offensive line's skill. His six touchdown passes were the most any quarterback had thrown on opening night. Brees and the Saints had made a loud statement: the Saints were the real deal, and they had one thing on their minds—winning!

And win is exactly what the Saints did.

Game after game, the Saints won. First it was four in a row, and then it was seven straight games. With each victory, the pressure mounted. Could the Saints complete a perfect season?

A perfect season in the NFL is when a team wins every regular season and playoff game—including the Super Bowl. It seemed a nearly impossible feat, but maybe—just maybe—it was something that Drew Brees could pull off. Only one team in NFL history had ever done it. In 1972, the Miami Dolphins won seventeen games in a row and Super Bowl VII. Any time a team started the season with a meaningful winning streak, the media began to speculate and whisper about whether they would challenge the 1972 Miami Dolphins record. By the time the Saints won their tenth game, those whispers had become a chorus—and they were even louder than usual because the Indianapolis Colts and Peyton Manning had started their season undefeated as well. For the first time, two NFL teams were both gunning for the elusive perfect season. And since the Saints were in the NFC and the Colts were in the AFC, the two excellent teams could potentially meet in a Super Bowl game.

One of Drew's best games that season was a rout of the New England Patriots, who had lost in the Super Bowl the previous season to Eli Manning and the New York Giants. In a matchup with quarterback Tom Brady, Drew stole the spotlight. It took him only eighteen passes to progress 237 yards, over 16 yards per pass! He also threw five touchdowns, over one and a half points per throw. That victory made eleven wins in a row, and the Saints clinched the number one ranking in the NFC South with five games left to play in the regular season. Unbelievable! The fans started calling their quarterback

Breesus—part Brees and part Jesus. That's how much the Who Dat Nation loved their quarterback.

The Saints were lucky to squeak past Washington with a close score of 33–30, and they again won a close game against the Falcons, 26–23. In early December, however, their luck unfortunately ran out when they lost to the Dallas Cowboys by seven points. While it was a hard loss, it might have been for the best: no more perfect season hopes meant no more outside pressure. The Colts lost for the first time that season a week later, and the media cycle calmed down. Now the Saints could focus on winning—except that they also lost the final games of the season to finish the year with a 13–3 record. Still, the Saints had never won thirteen games before. The last time they had even gotten close was more than ten years earlier, when they won twelve games in 1992.

During the last game of the season, the Saints rested many of their key players, and they went into the playoffs with a healthy team. Those last three losses left them hungry for a win, and they got one against the Arizona Cardinals in a 45–14 romp during the first round.

From the start, the NFC Championship game in New Orleans was a back-and-forth affair. In their first series, Adrian Peterson ran for a nineteen-yard touchdown for the Minnesota Vikings. The Saints played catch-up the rest of the half and managed to square the game away at fourteen by halftime. When the Saints finally took the lead at the beginning of the third quarter to make the game 21–14, the Vikings drove right down the field to even it up again. New Orleans would go up again at the start of the fourth on a five-yard touchdown to Reggie Bush, but the Saints defense couldn't keep Peterson contained, and he leveled the score again at 28–28. Both defenses made late stops to force the game into overtime. It was exhausting. Whoever made the first big mistake would lose the game. It was just too close to say who would come out victorious.

In overtime, Drew tried to push the Saints into field goal range, but he struggled to complete a pass. His nerves were taking over, and as he had in the past, he started pressing. He made fourteen incomplete passes that game, and five came from that last drive. Luckily, the Saints squeezed yards out of their running backs, who drove the team to the Vikings' twenty-two-yard line. Finally, kicker

Garrett Hartley made a forty-yard field goal five minutes into overtime. The Saints were on top! This win would send the Saints—and Drew—to their first Super Bowl ever. Drew was over the moon. But the Saints knew they'd have a hard game ahead against fierce competitors: Peyton Manning and the Colts.

New Orleans was buzzing in the weeks before the Super Bowl. Saints fans couldn't wait for the game. The Super Bowl would pit New Orleans's first son of football, Peyton Manning, against its adopted son, Drew Brees. Drew and Peyton were friends at this point, as Drew had become closer to the Manning family over the past season. Their friendship was going to help color the healthy rivalry the two men faced. While Drew had come into his own and was truly a great leader of the Saints, Peyton had also played great games all year—and on top of that, he was the league MVP. Every football fan knew that the Super Bowl game was going to be an epic battle.

Even Archie Manning, who had welcomed Drew into his city and had once been a Saints quarterback himself, was caught in the looming battle. In the end, he chose to root for his family.

"Of course I'm pulling for the Colts, one hundred

percent," said Archie. "You wouldn't be much of a parent—or a human being, for that matter—if you didn't pull for your kid. Anyone who has children would never ask that question."

After a 13–0 start to the season, Breesus had made believers out of everyone in New Orleans, and he had even converted people who hadn't enjoyed football before to the Who Dat Nation. In fact, in that past season, he had convinced practically everyone in the entire country that he had become a great quarterback. With his leadership on the field, Drew was the rock that the offense was built around. In his four seasons, he had achieved what no Saints quarterback before him had, breaking franchise and league records, and creating a winning culture within the Saints organization. He had elevated his status into the elite stratosphere of the position, and now he was on the verge of bringing home the team's first-ever Super Bowl championship. Even Archie understood how much the Saints quarterback had grown, and had said, "Drew owns New Orleans. He doesn't need my advice anymore."

If Drew was going to help the Saints win the Super Bowl and be worthy to hoist the coveted Vince Lombardi Trophy, he would need to outplay

Peyton Manning. He would have to play the best game he'd ever played. Drew knew this didn't necessarily mean playing the same way Peyton Manning did. Even trying to match Manning's stats would be a fool's errand. Brees had learned so much about himself as a player, and he knew what he could do—and what his faults were. He just needed to play his game and forget about trying to be as good as somebody else—that was what had made the Saints special all season long.

"That's exactly the trap I'm not going to fall into, which is trying to keep up with Peyton," Brees said days before the big game. "I know that Peyton is going to make his plays, and he's going to be Peyton, and that just means that I need to be me."

In the days before the game, most pundits and analysts in the media were picking the Colts to win. For most people, hearing that everyone thought their team was going to lose would be disheartening—but Drew wouldn't even have been playing football if he had listened to the doubters who had popped up throughout his career. He decided to believe in himself.

The Super Bowl is more than just a game. It's an entire day of commercials, media hype, sponsors selling their goods, parties, chips and wings—an entire day of football festivities. In fact, Super Bowl Sunday is the second-largest day for food consumption in the United States, right after Thanksgiving Day. There is pageantry to the game, with long player announcements and a huge halftime show. Families and friends huddle around a TV as over a hundred million people in the United States watch the game on Super Bowl Sunday.

To the players, however, it *is* another game— though perhaps one of the most important games of their careers. The field is the same length as it was during the regular season. They wear the same uniforms and pads, and the goalposts are just as high as they were in the last game they played. Drew Brees and the Saints got ready for the game by watching game tape after game tape, and practicing endlessly. Preparation for game day is a lot of work! Still, the process before playing in the Super Bowl is essentially the same as always. The main difference is that there is much more attention and pressure.

Sun Life Stadium, the home of the Dolphins and the University of Miami Hurricanes, hosted Super Bowl XLIV on February 7, 2010, in sunny Miami,

Florida. As Drew led the Saints onto the field, seventy-four thousand fans cheered and screamed, but he wasn't focused on them; he was focused on the game. He was in the zone.

The Colts defense had the Saints on their toes, though; the Saints started the game going three-and-out. Then Peyton Manning began to pick them apart. This was not a good sign. The Colts were moving the chains. Down in the red zone, Manning tried to find wide receiver Pierre Garçon on the right. He overthrew, and the Colts had to kick a field goal—they had opened the scoring quickly. It was going to be a long game if the Saints couldn't stop Manning.

But the Saints couldn't get anything started on the next series, and the Colts got the ball back. The Saints defense barely had a chance to rest before they were back on the field. That was when Colts running back Joseph Addai went to work. He scorched the Saints for a twenty-six-yard run, the longest of the game, into New Orleans's half of the field, before Manning hit Garçon with a laser in the end zone. And just like that, the Colts were up 10–0.

In the second quarter, Brees got it going. He

found his receivers on a few throws, and that opened the defense for his running backs to start blasting runs. The Saints were deep in Colts territory looking for the touchdown when All-Pro linebacker Dwight Freeney sacked Brees on third and three for a seven-yard loss. The Saints had to put some points on the board before they fell even farther behind, so they settled for a forty-six-yard field goal. The game looked like it was going to get away from them, but their defense forced a three-and-out, and gave the ball right back to the offense.

Drew started to see the Colts defense more clearly. The Saints moved the ball to the three with a fresh set of downs, but a penalty and a stout Colts defense kept the Saints out of the end zone. On fourth down, Saints head coach Sean Payton chose to give up the guaranteed points and try for the touchdown. The Saints were stuffed at the one-yard line, however, and got nothing. After stonewalling the Colts a second time, the Saints were able to put three more points on the board before halftime, and cut the score to 10–6. Nothing had gone the Saints' way that half, but they were down only four points, thanks to their excellent defense.

The Saints went in after the half and made some

serious adjustments to their offense. They started by kicking an unexpected onside kick; Drew attacked the left side, then cut the ball underneath and inside. With the Colts defense on their heels, Drew hit running back Pierre Thomas on a screen pass up the middle for a sixteen-yard touchdown, and the Saints had their first lead of the game. Manning responded, forcing the New Orleans defense into some bad coverage by going no huddle for the next series. Five yards, seven yards, two yards—then came a dagger for twenty-seven yards.

The Saints defense couldn't get their feet set. Manning sprayed balls all over the field, and New Orleans couldn't stop him. Manning had the Colts four yards from goal before Addai pounded the rock into the end zone, allowing the Colts to retake the lead. The Saints hit another field goal toward the end of the third quarter and with fifteen minutes to play. The score was 17–16, in favor of the Colts. It was incredibly close, and it seemed that everything Drew had worked for—everything he'd fought for since high school—was within reach. But Peyton Manning and the Colts were also hungry for the win. Whoever wanted it more and played hardest in the fourth quarter would win the game.

On the first series of the fourth quarter, the Colts drove the ball to the New Orleans thirty-three-yard line before shanking a field goal that would have extended their one-point lead. It was Drew's turn on the next series. Everything went quiet, and Drew began to play like he'd never played before. He connected on six straight passes to lead the Saints into the red zone, before hitting tight end Jeremy Shockey on slant, making an incredible pass that went diagonally across the field, for the touchdown.

Coach Payton made the call for a two-point conversion. The play called for wide receiver Lance Moore to run a quick out along the goal line in the right flat. Once Moore made his move, Drew snapped the ball and threw it onto Moore's outside shoulder, where he snagged the ball out of the air and rolled over, extending his arms to break the plane of the end zone. As he hit the ground, however, the defender knocked the ball free, and the pass was ruled incomplete by the line judge. It was a call that could make or break the entire game. The Saints angrily challenged the call on the field—and after reviewing the play, the referee overturned it, ruling the play a touchdown and giving the Saints a seven-point lead.

An important rule for players to follow against Peyton Manning was to never give him time. Given time, Manning would find a weakness in the Saints defense and score. With over five minutes on the clock, Manning went to work. Going no huddle, the Colts walked the ball down the field. It looked like Manning was going to tie the game and force overtime, but cornerback Tracy Porter jumped wide receiver Reggie Wayne's route. He had intercepted the ball, and he took it all the way—seventy-four yards—to score a touchdown. Instead of letting Manning tie things up, the Saints defense had stepped up and shut the door on the game. After the extra point, the Saints led, and ended the game with a score of 31–17. New Orleans had won!

"Just to think of the road we've all traveled, the adversity we've all faced," Drew said after his amazing performance. "It's unbelievable. I mean, are you kidding me? Four years ago, who would have ever thought this would be happening? Eighty-five percent of the city was under water. Most people left not knowing if New Orleans would ever come back, or if the organization would ever come back.

"We just all looked at one another and said, 'We're going to rebuild together. We are going to lean on each other.' That's what we've done the last four years, and this is the culmination in all that belief," Drew continued.

The Saints had played an outstanding game, and for Drew, the Super Bowl win was a dream realized after years of endless hard work and proving his doubters wrong. He was awarded the Super Bowl's Most Valuable Player for his performance. Out of thirty-nine pass attempts, he had completed thirty-two, which tied with New England Patriots quarterback Tom Brady for the most completions in a Super Bowl. He threw for 288 yards and two touchdowns. He was the picture of an on-field general. He had done what no other Saints quarterback had done before him: he had helped deliver the ultimate football prize—a Super Bowl championship.

"We play for so much more than ourselves," said Drew, with his brown hair matted to his forehead. "We played for our city. We played for the entire Gulf Coast region. We played for the entire Who Dat Nation that has been behind us every step of the way."

DREW BREES

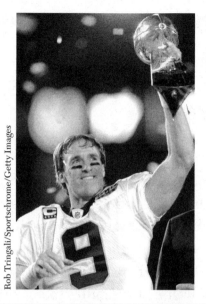

Rob Tringali/Sportschrome/Getty Images

DREW HOLDS UP THE VINCE LOMBARDI TROPHY AFTER DEFEATING THE
INDIANAPOLIS COLTS IN SUPER BOWL XLIV.

CHAPTER SEVENTEEN
2010-2011

TITLE DEFENSE

The 2010 off-season was a strange time in the NFL. In 2008, the NFL owners had voted to change the collective bargaining agreement within two years. The collective bargaining agreement established the boundaries and regulations for trading football players, as well as for signing them to new teams. The agreement also controlled working conditions around the league. When the NFL Players Association and the owners couldn't reach a new collective bargaining agreement before the 2010 season, the league was allowed to operate freely, without the limitations of a salary cap. This meant teams could retain more of their veteran players than they would have been able to under the normal rules. It also turned many would-be unrestricted free agents into restricted free agents, giving those players less bargaining power as they negotiated with teams. All in all, the landscape of that off-season was drastically changed from previous years.

The uncapped year allowed New Orleans to keep safety Roman Harper, running back Pierre Thomas, and wide receiver Lance Moore, but they were each forced to play at a considerably reduced salary. They all had been key players in the championship run, and some of them were now being asked to play for less money than their backups were making. The tension between players and management was evident at the start of training camp that season.

The Saints went into their title defense still loaded with talent and ready to make a deep run into the playoffs. The season got off on the right foot with wins against Minnesota and San Francisco, but the Saints then stumbled for a few games. They were sitting at 4–3 when they rattled off six consecutive wins, ending the season 11–5. Normally, that record would win the South, but that year the Saints were two games behind the Atlanta Falcons, and they went into the playoffs as one of the wild cards rather than a division leader.

In another unusual situation that season, the Seattle Seahawks had won the NFC West with a record of 7–9, becoming the first team to qualify for the playoffs with a record under .500 in a full season of play. Despite having won four more games than Seattle that season, the Saints traveled to Qwest Field (soon to be renamed CenturyLink Field), home of the Seattle Seahawks, for the first round of the playoffs.

Against all odds, the Seahawks beat the Saints 41–36. Drew threw for 404 yards and two touchdowns, but the Seahawks rode their home-field advantage. The loss was demoralizing. Drew and the Saints were out of the playoffs in the very first round. This was not the way they wanted their season to end, especially coming off an incredible Super Bowl win. Still, Brees and the Saints had much to be proud of. They were one of the most talented teams in the league, and on top of that, the Saints had made it to back-to-back playoff appearances for the first time since the early 1990s. Even though they had lost early on, they were still breaking records.

Drew had also had a great year since winning the Super Bowl in February. In recognition of everything he had done, he received the *Sports Illustrated* Sportsman of the Year and the Associated Press Athlete of the Year awards. Each was only given to one athlete per year, and it was a great honor for Drew to receive both simultaneously.

"I've always tried to visualize myself in that position of being considered one of the best, and winning championships," said Drew. "Certainly the way you're perceived, the way people talk about you, the kind of category they put you in—that stuff changes and it's flattering, certainly humbling."

In winning those awards, Drew Brees joined an amazing list of athletes that included Muhammad Ali, Sandy Koufax, Wayne Gretzky, and Michael Jordan. He was in great company! The awards also confirmed Drew's place among the elite athletes of the modern era. But no matter how prestigious and wonderful those awards were, they meant nothing in comparison to the excitement of a new addition to his family. In the middle of that season, Drew and his wife, Brittany, had welcomed their second baby boy. Bowen Christopher Brees was born on October 19, 2010.

Before Drew, the Saints had been in a playoff drought, without much for the Who Dat Nation to rally behind and cheer for. However, Drew helped lift the Saints out of their playoff drought and turned them into NFL champions. He also helped change the expectations of a team that, before his arrival, had made the playoffs only once in fourteen seasons. Now that New Orleans knew the feeling of being Super Bowl champions, they'd strive harder to get back there again.

Drew would lead the Saints to a third straight playoff appearance and a 13–3 record in 2011. The Saints won eight straight games to end the season, but after beating the Lions in the first round of the playoffs, they lost to the San Francisco 49ers, ending their run at another Super Bowl championship. The 2011 season, however, was still a very special season for Drew Brees.

That season, Drew was named the FedEx Air Player of the Year for the fourth time, and he smashed Dan Marino's record for most passing yards in a single season by 392 yards. Drew threw for an amazing 5,476 yards over the course of the regular season. That record had stood for twenty-seven years.

Drew also set the mark for the highest completion percentage for a season with 71.2 percent and 468 completions. Over the course of that season, he showed that he could be the model of efficiency. He averaged 342.3 yards per game and threw for over

300 yards in thirteen of sixteen games, and over 400 yards twice. He threw forty-six touchdowns and was intercepted only fourteen times. That is an average of 2.86 touchdowns per game, with less than one interception per game. Another way to look at that is that he averaged twenty points per game. It's no wonder that, with Drew's leadership and record-breaking year, the Saints were able to win so many games. But as wonderful the 2011 season was, things were about to get a lot more complicated for the Saints.

CHAPTER EIGHTEEN
2012

BOUNTYGATE

Rumors of a league investigation began to surface in early 2012, and when it was time to begin the draft, it was all anyone seemed to be talking about. Truth be told, there had been rumors swirling around the Saints for many years, and the NFL had started investigating rumors about the Saints' defensive players. Many people seemed to think that the athletes had received bonuses in the form of cash or goods for hard tackles, or for intentionally injuring opposing players, as early as 2010. This kind of behavior is not only morally wrong and a display of bad sportsmanship, but it is also against NFL rules. Over the course of multiple seasons, opposing teams had reported "dirty" play by the Saints to the NFL head office. This was a problem that the league had to look into further.

The NFL investigation committee, headed by former commissioner Paul Tagliabue, uncovered evidence that some of the Saints defensive players had in fact been paid to hurt or hit certain opposing players. It was an illegal bounty system that had been established and eventually overseen by defensive coordinator Gregg Williams. It seemed that head coach Sean Payton was aware of the bounty program, too, as was general manager Mickey Loomis.

Even the Saints owner, Tom Benson, knew about it. When Benson had found out about the bounty program, however, he immediately instructed Loomis to discontinue it. However, Loomis did not. In fact, the investigation found that Loomis took no steps to stop the program at all, just as Coach Payton was found to have known of the program and had taken no steps to end it. Four players on the Saints team were also found to be heavily involved: Jonathan Vilma, Anthony Hargrove, Will Smith, and Scott Fujita.

In the spring of 2012, current NFL commissioner Roger Goodell came down hard on the Saints. Gregg Williams received the harshest of penalties: he was suspended indefinitely and banned from even applying for reinstatement for at least one year. Only Goodell could decide to lift the suspension. Essentially, there was a chance that Williams would never be allowed to participate in football again.

By this time, Williams had already left the Saints and was the new defensive coordinator for the St. Louis Rams. When he was suspended, the Rams were left without a defensive coordinator. In a way, Williams's actions hurt the Rams, too, even though they'd had nothing to do with the scandal.

Sean Payton was suspended for the entire 2012 season. This was a big deal—not only for the Saints, but for all of football—because he was the first head coach ever to have been suspended by the league. Loomis was banned from the first eight games that season. Vilma was also suspended for the entire 2012 season, while Hargrove, Smith, and Fujita were suspended eight, four, and three games respectively. The Saints were stripped of their second-round draft picks in 2012 and 2013, and also fined $500,000.

The Saints appointed linebackers coach Joe Vitt as the interim head coach, but he had also received a six-game suspension because of the scandal. This forced the Saints to have offensive line coach Aaron Kromer lead the team in the meantime.

The Saints stuck together through the rough patch. Drew Brees testified that the NFL had gotten the evidence wrong and that the bounty system did not exist. It took over a year for the truth to come out. Jonathan Vilma was adamant that he never took part in the bounty program, and Drew believed him. For Drew, it seemed impossible that his teammates would intentionally hurt other players. They had all worked and trained too hard, and did not need to rely on cheating. They had too much pride in the game and their team to allow such a bounty system to exist. It became clear that Commissioner Goodell had been too fast to judge the team and too harsh in his penalties. By September 7, all players' suspensions were overturned on appeal, and by the end of the 2012 season, Paul Tagliabue upheld the coaches' suspensions, but vacated the players' suspensions altogether.

Even though these penalties were overturned, the scandal hung over the team like a dark cloud. The 2012 season was, for all intents and purposes, lost before it had even started. Despite the scandal, Drew believed in the Saints, and he agreed to a new five-year, $100-million contract prior to the start of the season. This was one of the NFL's richest contracts—it that meant he would be staying with the team through the 2016 season. At the end of that contract, he would be thirty-eight years old and in his sixteenth season in the NFL. He was grateful for the new deal and the faith the management was putting in him to continue to lead the team. In a statement after the deal was announced, Drew expressed his love for the organization, his team, and the city of New Orleans. He thanked the owners for the opportunity and ended with words showing once again how hardworking he was, saying, "Now I need to go earn it."

With all of the new coaches and media presence, the 2012 season was one of Drew's most difficult. One of the best parts of that year was the birth of his third son, Callen Christian Brees, on August 15. Even though it was a tough season for Drew, he was still very good, and he had been nothing if not consistent—but the atmosphere in the locker room had changed. The team dynamic had been altered, the scandal fresh in everyone's minds. On top of that, the team sorely missed Payton's coaching and strategy.

The Saints ended the season with a 7–9 record, missing the playoffs for the first time since 2009. Drew started all sixteen games and threw for over 5,000 yards for the second season in a row. His record for throwing at least one touchdown in a game came to an end at fifty-four games that year.

It's an NFL record that still stands. He had forty-three touchdowns with only nineteen interceptions. All in all, it was another great season for him, but under the new defensive coordinator, the Saints defense wasn't as good as it once had been. In 2012, the Saints defense allowed an average 440 yards per game, the worst all-time average in the NFL. No matter how great a player Drew Brees was, football was still a team sport.

DREW BREES CATCHES A PASS FROM MICKEY MOUSE AT THE ESPN WIDE WORLD OF SPORTS COMPLEX AT WALT DISNEY WORLD IN 2013. DREW WAS THERE TO CONDUCT HIS DREW BREES PASSING ACADEMY, WHERE THE PROCEEDS WOULD BENEFIT THE BREES DREAM FOUNDATION.

CHAPTER NINETEEN
2013

REBOUND YEAR

The Saints had paid the price during the 2012 season. The penalties had been served. The fines had been paid. The distractions outside of football were gone, and it was time to get back to doing what Drew and the Saints did best: playing football and winning as many games as they could!

To fix the defensive unit that did not perform well in 2012, the Saints brought in Rob Ryan as the new defensive coordinator. With most of their strong players together for another season, the offense was set to make another push to the playoffs and, hopefully, the Super Bowl.

The season started well. The Saints beat their rivals, the Atlanta Falcons, in Coach Payton's return from his suspension. They went on to win their first five games, earning their first loss at the hands of Tom Brady and the New England Patriots the week before their bye. By the time New Orleans completed the season sweep of Atlanta in late November, the Saints were 9–2—and they were in first place. Payton and Brees had picked up right where they had left off during the 2011 season.

The worst loss came at the hands of the Seattle Seahawks. The Seahawks had the best defense during the 2013 season, and for the first time since the last game of 2011, Drew was held to under two hundred yards passing. The defensive backs for Seattle blanketed the Saints receivers, batted down balls, and generally created havoc for the Saints offense.

The Saints' prolific aerial attack was completely grounded. Drew went twenty-three for thirty-eight for 147 yards—not quite what Saints fans were used to from their signal caller. In many ways, the Seahawks did exactly what the Saints had been doing to their opponents for years. Seattle played a physically tough brand of football on defense and offense, behind five-foot-eleven-inch quarterback Russell Wilson. They had consistently accurate passing against the Saints and played a tough running game.

The Saints split the last four games to end the season and come in second in the NFC South, behind the Carolina Panthers. They had once again made the playoffs.

The Saints had never won a road playoff game, and the Eagles had only lost once in the last two years at home, so the first-round matchup in Philadelphia was not expected to go well. The game would pit Drew against Eagles quarterback Nick Foles, who also happened to have attended Westlake High School.

It was a tough game from the kickoff. Drew could get them into the red zone, but he couldn't quite move the ball past the goal line. The Saints were one for four inside the twenty-yard line. Drew was tackled inside the five-yard line, one of two sacks of the night. Luckily for him, recently signed kicker Shayne Graham was happy to put the points on the board for the team. Graham connected on thirty-six- and forty-six-yard field goals in the second quarter. They were down by only one point at halftime, with a score of 7–6. It was still anyone's game.

That was when Drew started to play with the kind of skill that had helped to make him a household name. He and running back Mark Ingram moved the chains, getting a first down that allowed them to go deep into Philly territory. Drew found wide receiver Lance Moore over the middle for a twenty-four-yard touchdown. The Saints defense would force the Eagles to go three-and-out, and the Saints capitalized by putting three more points on the board, taking a 20–7 lead with twenty minutes left in the game.

The Eagles came storming back and outscored the Saints 17–3 over the next ten minutes, taking the lead at 24–23 with just under five minutes left to play. Drew knew that he needed to stall if he wanted to win. If he scored with too much time left on the clock, he would give Foles a chance to move the Eagles into field goal range, but Drew still had to make sure he got close enough to score or kick a field goal. Running back Darren Sproles made it much easier on his quarterback when he returned a kickoff to the Saints. A penalty on the play moved the ball to midfield. Now Brees could go to work!

The Saints started to go with a heavy run package, but the Eagles were dropping their linebackers and stacking men in the box. Brees calmly and coolly hit Marques Colston for six yards. That play forced the defense to respect the pass and drop more men into coverage. On the third and three, Brees took the ball himself and got the first down at the Eagles' twenty-four-yard line—crucially, this kept the clock running. After two more plays on the ground, Brees would run for a first down and then stall the clock with another run for no gain, before taking the timeout with three seconds left on the clock. The quarterback known for his passing game had just exploited Philly's defense on the ground. Graham kicked a thirty-two-yard field goal as time expired. The Saints' playoff drought ended right there in Philadelphia.

The Saints would lose their rematch and end their season the next week to the eventual Super Bowl champion Seattle Seahawks. However, the team had successfully bounced back after the big scandal. This was more than Drew could have asked for.

CHAPTER TWENTY 2014 AND BEYOND

THE FUTURE

Drew Brees had truly come a long way. It was almost impossible to imagine that, at one point, he had considered quitting football. Fresh out of high school, he had easily been the most overlooked recruit because of his height—he was perhaps the most undervalued college recruit of all time. Most of the country did not see Drew's best qualities until he worked hard to prove his talent and skill. Many programs that could have signed him would probably have done so in a heartbeat had they realized what an incredible, tough, hardworking quarterback and team leader he would turn out to be.

But how do you grade Drew's work ethic, his desire to win, or his unflagging character? It's impossible to put a value on heart. Even as a high school student, he had a lot of it, and a lot of passion for the game and playing it right. Because of his heart and his undeniable spirit, Drew helped redefine the prototype of the modern-day quarter-back. Before, it was practically unthinkable that a quarterback could be less than six feet tall. Only a few such players had made it to the big time, but thanks to Drew Brees, many successful quarter-backs have been able to enter the professional league as well. Russell Wilson, for example, is five feet eleven inches, while Johnny Manziel stands at six feet. More scouts and teams now look past the height issue, focusing instead on what quarterbacks have done—and can do—on the field. This is largely thanks to Drew Brees.

Drew has overcome every obstacle that has been placed in front of him. He has climbed to the top of the NFL by working hard on the field and off it. He stays humble, remembering the lessons instilled in him by his family and by his faith. He is a family man who takes pride in his wife and children, three sons and a daughter (Rylen Judith Brees was born in August 2014). He is dedicated to community service, and some of his best work has been off the field as he gives back to his community and his fans. In 2003, Drew and his wife, Brittany, started the Brees Dream Foundation in order to help people with cancer and families in need. The foundation has donated over $22 million to charities across the world, including charities in the cities and states he has lived in during his football career, in Indiana, California, and Louisiana. He has showed his gratitude to the city that adopted him by helping New Orleans rebuild after the devastation of Hurricane Katrina. He has also participated in USO tours to visit with the men and women of the US armed forces who serve overseas.

Today, Drew holds many NFL records and franchise records. He has been to the Pro Bowl every year since 2008; he has his Super Bowl MVP, and his team has its Vince Lombardi Trophy. Many believe that he is all but guaranteed a spot in the NFL Hall of Fame. Drew could retire today as one of the best at his position—but he won't.

Drew Brees never gave up on himself. He never let those who didn't believe in him dictate who he was and who he could be—and he never quit. He has only won one Super Bowl so far, but if anyone were to tell him that he would never be able to win another—well, anyone could just guess what would happen next.

Ronald Martinez/Getty Images

DREW BREES CELEBRATES WITH HIS SON BAYLEN AFTER WINNING THE SUPER BOWL IN 2010.

TURN THE PAGE
FOR MORE
FUN FACTS!

DREW'S AWARDS AND RECORDS

Drew had very different experiences on his Westlake, Purdue, and NFL teams, but wherever he played, he played his best. Take a look at some of the records he's held and awards he's won over his amazing career.

HIGH SCHOOL

16–0 perfect season

5A State Championship

3,528 yards and 31 touchdowns

COLLEGE

NCAA record holder for longest
touchdown pass (99 yards)

Big Ten record holder for passing yards in a career
(11,792 yards from 1997 to 2000)

Big Ten record holder for single-season
touchdowns (39 in 1998) and for career
touchdowns (90 from 1997 to 2000)

Big Ten record holder for single-season
completions (361 in 1998) and for career
completions (1,026 from 1997 to 2000)

Big Ten record holder for single-season attempts
(569 in 1998; tied with Curtis Painter) and for
career attempts (1,678 from 1997 to 2000)

Maxwell Award (nation's top player) (2000)

Academic All-American of the Year (2000)

Two-time Heisman finalist—finished fourth in
1999 and third in 2000

First-ever Socrates Award in 1999 for the nation's
finest athlete scholar

Big Ten Offensive
Player of the Year (1998, 2000)

Alamo Bowl MVP (1998)

Outback Bowl MVP (1999)

PROFESSIONAL

Super Bowl XLIV Champion (2009 season)

Super Bowl XLIV MVP (2009 season)

NFC MVP (2008, 2009)

AP NFL Offensive Player of the Year (2008, 2011)

Walter Payton Man of the Year (2006; joint
winner with LaDainian Tomlinson)

Bart Starr Man of the Year (2011)

ESPY Sportsman/Athlete of the Year (2010)

NFC Champion (2009)

Pro Bowl (2004, 2006, 2008–2014)

First-team All-Pro (2006)

Second-team All-Pro (2008, 2009, 2011)

NFL Alumni Quarterback of the Year
(2006, 2009)

AP NFL Comeback Player of the Year (2004)

Bert Bell Award (2009)

NFL record for most consecutive games with at least 1 touchdown pass (54 games)

NFL record for highest completion percentage
(71.2% in 2011)

NFL record for most 4,000-yard passing seasons (9)

NFL record for most 300-plus-yard passing games
in a season (13)

NFL record for most completions in a season (468)

DREW'S SEASONS BY THE NUMBERS— COMPLETIONS & ATTEMPTS

With the Chargers and Saints, Drew has had great season after great season. Check out these stats!

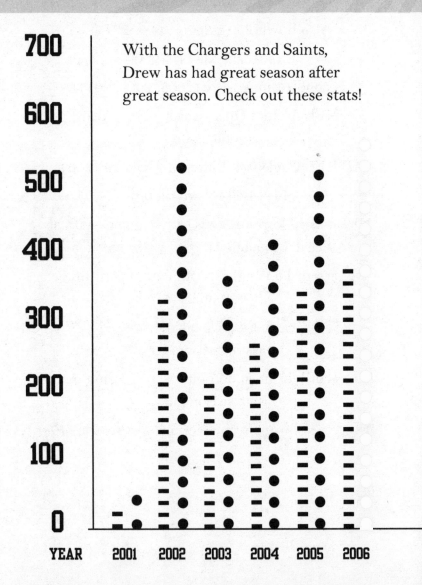

YEAR 2001 2002 2003 2004 2005 2006

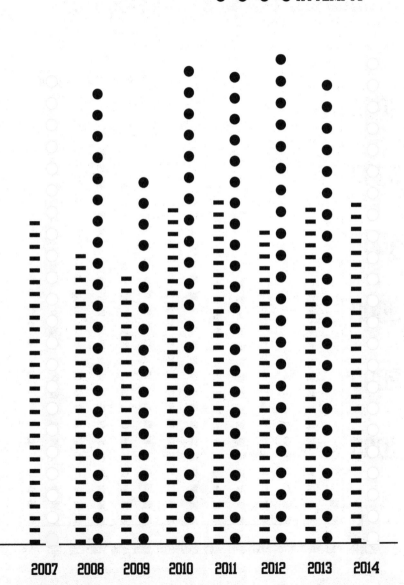

COMPLETIONS
ATTEMPTS

2007 2008 2009 2010 2011 2012 2013 2014

DREW'S SEASONS BY THE NUMBERS—RUSHING YARDS & TOUCHDOWNS

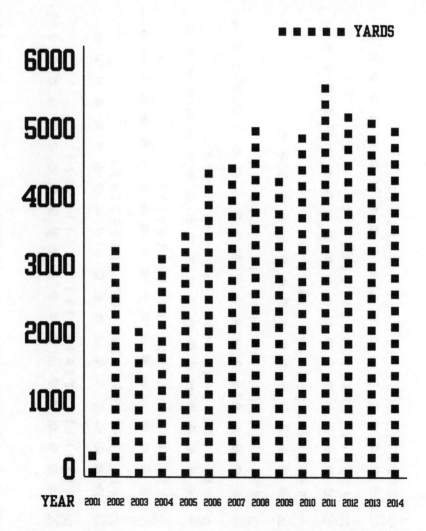

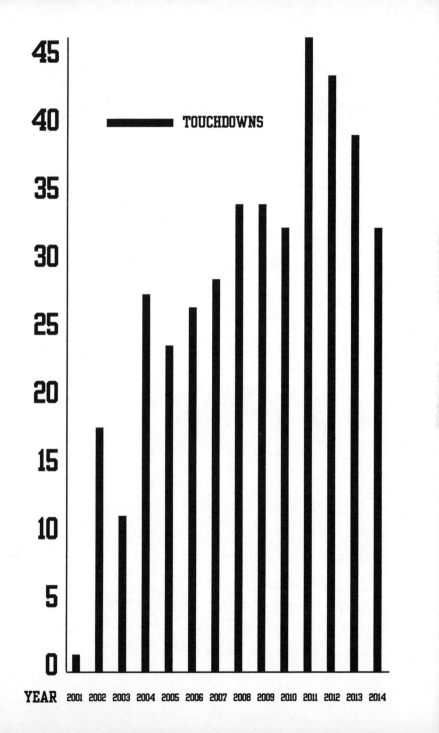

DREW'S SEASONS BY THE NUMBERS (CONT.)

COMPLETIONS	ATTEMPTS
2001—15	2001—27
2002—320	2002—526
2003—205	2003—356
2004—262	2004—400
2005—323	2005—500
2006—356	2006—554
2007—440	2007—652
2008—413	2008—635
2009—363	2009—514
2010—448	2010—658
2011—468	2011—657
2012—422	2012—670
2013—446	2013—650
2014—456	2014—659

YARDS	TOUCHDOWNS
2001—221	2001—1
2002—3,284	2002—17
2003—2,108	2003—11
2004—3,159	2004—27
2005—3,576	2005—24
2006—4,418	2006—26
2007—4,423	2007—28
2008—5,069	2008—34
2009—4,388	2009—34
2010—4,620	2010—33
2011—5,476	2011—46
2012—5,177	2012—43
2013—5,162	2013—39
2014—4,952	2014—33

DREW'S TOUCHDOWN STREAKS

Drew holds the record for all-time consecutive games* with at least one touchdown pass at fifty-four games. And not only does he hold that record, but going into the 2015 season, he's on another streak that ties him for sixth place. Here's how he stacks up against other top-ranked quarterbacks:

DREW BREES
New Orleans Saints

10/18/2009–11/25/2012

TOM BRADY
New England Patriots

9/12/2010–9/29/2013

PEYTON MANNING
Indianapolis Colts and Denver Broncos

11/21/2010–11/30/2014

JOHNNY UNITAS
Baltimore Colts

12/9/1956–12/4/1960

TONY ROMO
Dallas Cowboys

10/1/2012–11/23/2014

BRETT FAVRE
Green Bay Packers

10/20/2002–11/29/2004

DREW BREES
New Orleans Saints

12/9/2012–PRESENT**

DAN MARINO
Miami Dolphins

11/10/1985–11/22/1987

BEN ROETHLISBERGER
Pittsburgh Steelers

9/9/2012–9/7/2014

* This "official streak" is defined as a player passing for touchdown passes in consecutive games in which the player participated (during the regular season). So if a quarterback has to sit out a game or games for an injury, the record clock pauses and picks back up when that quarterback next steps onto the field.
** going into the 2015 season

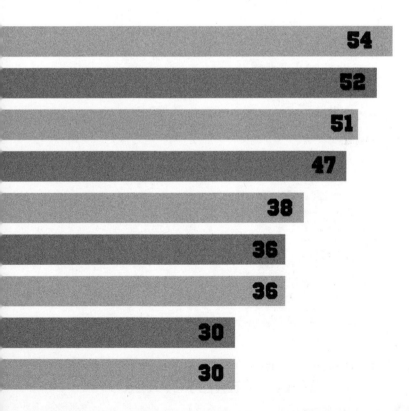